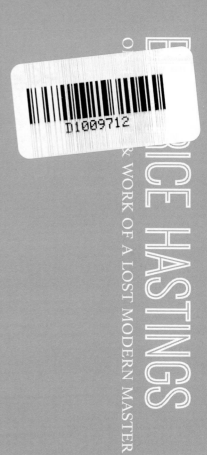

BEATRICE HASTINGS

ON THE LIFE & WORK OF A LOST MODERN MASTER

BEATRICE HASTINGS

ON THE LIFE & WORK OF A LOST MODERN MASTER

Edited by Benjamin Johnson and Erika Jo Brown

ISBN: 978-0-9641454-8-1

Published by Pleiades Press & *Gulf Coast*

Department of English
University of Central Missouri
Warrensburg, Missouri 64093

Department of English
University of Houston
Houston, Texas 77204

Distributed by Small Press Distribution (SPD) and to
subscribers of *Pleiades: Literature in Context* and
Gulf Coast: A Journal of Literature and Fine Arts.

Series, cover, and interior design by Martin Rock.
Cover photograph courtesy of the H.P.B. Library in Toronto.

2 4 6 8 9 7 5 3 1
First Printing, 2016

The Unsung Masters Series brings the work of great, out-of-print, little-known writers to new readers. Each volume in the series includes a large selection of the author's original writing, as well as essays on the writer, interviews with people who knew the writer, photographs, and ephemera. The curators of the Unsung Masters Series are always interested in suggestions for future volumes.

Invaluable financial support for this project has been provided by the National Endownment for the Arts, the Cynthia Woods Mitchell Center for the Arts, and the Missouri Arts Council, a state agency. Our immense gratitude to these organizations.

THE UNSUNG MASTERS SERIES

gulf coast
A JOURNAL OF LITERATURE AND FINE ARTS + PLEIADES
PRESS

CONTENTS

FICTION

IMPRESSIONS OF PARIS

MEMOIRS

GALLERY

ESSAYS ON BEATRICE HASTINGS

INTRODUCTION

INTRODUCTION

SHE was so committed to pseudonyms that even Beatrice Hastings is one. Born Emily Alice Beatrice Haigh in 1879,[1] she spent her childhood in South Africa before eventually finding success as a writer in London and Paris in the early twentieth century. From 1907 to 1920, her work appeared in *The New Age*, a London weekly known for its socialist political bent, its reviews of contemporary art and literature, and its no-holds-barred culture of internal debate. She wrote under a dizzying array of pen names: as Beatrice Tina, she was an aesthete, poet, and critic of restrictive roles for women; as D. Triformis, she was a withering essayist and opponent of the suffrage movement (and, for that matter, an opponent of Beatrice Tina); as T.K.L., she wrote dense, high-spirited parodies; as Alice Morning, she was a chatty, digressive diarist of Paris during the First World War; and as Beatrice Hastings, she combined a bit of all these personalities to craft herself into a skeptical, curious, and chameleonic public intellectual.

And then, she vanished. She published a handful of books in her later life and tried her hand at starting up two different periodicals, but none was a success, and all went out of print after their initial appearance. As the story of the literary 1910's came to be told by the victors and anthologists, she was shuffled to the side, and her death in 1943 went largely unremarked. She has appeared from time to time in a stray footnote or middle chapter in the biographies of her lovers, collaborators, and sparring partners, including Amedeo Modigliani, Katherine Mansfield, Raymond Radiguet, and A.R. Orage. She has even been portrayed on screen in a handful of films about Modigliani (most recently and ludicrously in a 2004 Andy Garcia vehicle). The South African novelist Stephen Gray published a monumental, meticulously researched biography of her in 2004, but it is very difficult to find.[2] Scholars have, on occasion and with increasing frequency, presented her as a piece of a larger cultural narrative: Lucy Delap in her discussion of feminism and anti-feminism in the early twentieth century; John Carswell in his book about writers attached to *The New Age*; Robert Scholes in his account of writers who also served as models for modernist painters. And millions of people have strolled past Modigliani's portraits of her in museums around the world, pausing to take in the visage of a woman who has, for a century, been hiding in plain sight in the middle of the story of modernism.

It took her a while, though, to make it to the middle of anything. South Africa was a British colony on the brink of the first Anglo-Boer War when Hastings was born into a large, prosperous family. She spent her childhood shuttling between South Africa and boarding school in England, and while her autobiographical sketches indicate a deep affection for the African landscapes of her youth, her ambition and restlessness took her abroad. In a caption she scribbled on a photograph of herself at age 19 with one shoulder provocatively exposed, she describes herself as being "in full revolt."

What exactly happened to Hastings in her young adult years is tricky to discern, in part because Hastings only ever wrote about those years in *Pages from an Unpublished Novel*, a serial work she wrote for *The New Age* which mixes fiction, autobiography, and even literary criticism in ways that make verifiable biographical "truth" difficult to nail down. Gray establishes beyond a shadow of a doubt that Hastings married a much older man named Edward Chamberlain in 1897. The marriage was not happy, and after the couple moved to England together, they parted ways. Hastings remained in England while Chamberlain returned to South Africa, where he died a short time later.[3] A few years later, she married a boxer named Lachlan Thomson, and though she did not live with him for long, she apparently never legally divorced him either, and "Mrs. Lachlan Thomson" is the name on her death certificate.[4]

At some point in her young adulthood, she gave birth to a child that died in infancy. Though Hastings never recorded the name of this child in any of her works, the experience colors much of her early writing in a variety of genres. Inexperienced women duped into unhappy motherhood is a frequent theme in her fiction, most notably her 1909 novella *Whited Sepulchres*.[5] The topic of maternity is also a central concern of *Woman's Worst Enemy: Woman*, a 1909 collection of essays Hastings put together after her *New Age* essay "Woman as State Creditor" generated a great deal of correspondence. *Woman's Worst Enemy* is one of the most fiery works of a fiery career, as Hastings bristles against the narrow paths available to women, most notably the path of motherhood:

> Never, at any time of my whole existence, did I want to become a mother. As a very young girl the knowledge of the process shocked and repelled me, and I could never hear a reference to birth without experiencing nausea. Among visions of beauty and delight I dwelled in my inner mind until the rude shock of knowledge showed me a yawning pit of human pain; and this abyss, I was told, was the way all women had to go.

In her essay in this book, Erin Kingsley argues persuasively that Hastings's writing about motherhood should be understood within the framework of a much broader early-twentieth-century debate in which arguments about eugenics and the potential military consequences of a declining British population made parturition and child-rearing topics of political concern. However, Hastings's writing on maternity is not of exclusively historical interest. Though the parameters of the debate have shifted over the past hundred years, Hastings's insistence on giving voice to the experience of women who do not want to be mothers has contemporary analogues in genres from the novel to the blog, and she is prescient in her awareness that the modern expansion of women's domestic and sexual options would make maternity a charged and recurrent topic of modern political debate.

In 1906, Hastings met A. R. Orage in London at a Theosophical Society meeting and, as she joked three decades later, "Aphrodite... amused herself at our expense."[6] Within a year, the two were living together, and would continue to do so for most of the next seven years. Orage, like Hastings, was an outsider to London political and intellectual life: he had grown up in a working class family in Northern England, and was educated at a small teacher's college in Culham.[7] He also resembled Hastings in his capacious intellectual interests. Over the course of his career he published books on economics, literature, and Nietzsche. Soon after he met Hastings, Orage and his friend Holbrook Jackson took over *The New Age*, and by the end of 1907, Hastings was writing for the magazine. Like everyone on the small staff of the paper, Hastings wore a variety of hats. She started out writing on political topics—notably capital punishment and "the woman question"—but within two years she was also publishing poetry, fiction, and literary criticism, and she also did much of the literary editing. She collaborated on satirical pieces with Katherine Mansfield, with whom she had an intense relationship and equally intense falling out.[8]

Hastings's work mostly appeared under pseudonyms or anonymously. In an appendix to a memoir, she lists fifteen different pen names, and hints that there were others.[9] Her motives for obscuring the scope of her contribution to *The New Age* are not entirely clear—she wrote decades later that "I thought it better for the paper...I cared for nothing but the paper, that was my life."[10] Hastings was certainly not the only *New Age* writer to use pen names (Orage, for instance, wrote many pieces anonymously or as R.H.C.), and one suspects that obscuring authorship might have been a strategy to make it appear that the weekly had more contributors than it actually did. Hastings, however, had more *New Age* pseudonyms than anyone else, and she used them to fascinating aesthetic effect. She created distinctive authorial voices and occasionally staged arguments with herself, most notably in an exchange included in this book in which D. Triformis in the essay "Women and Freedom" criticizes Beatrice Tina's "Woman as State Creditor," only to be replied to the next week in a letter by "Beatrice (Tina) Hastings."[11]

As that self-exchange indicates, Hastings's beliefs about women's suffrage—probably the most contentious political issue in Britain in the years leading up to the war—were complicated, shifting, and at times contradictory. Carey Snyder's essay in this book examines the ways that Hastings used her pen names to approach the question of suffrage from multiple angles. Snyder also traces the trajectory of Hastings's evolving opinions on the matter which, broadly speaking, move from supporting suffrage and feminism while writing as Beatrice Tina in 1908 and 1909 to opposing militant suffrage and the upper-class leaders of the Women's Social and Political Union (WSPU) while writing as D. Triformis in 1910. In later years, Hastings argued that women are unfit for politics or involvement in the war effort even as she was scathingly critical of writers who tried to pigeonhole women into traditional social roles. (Her biting review of the novel *Tante* in the July 22, 1915 "Impressions of Paris" is a good example of the latter.) Hastings's views on feminism are difficult to sum up, especially at the remove of a hundred years. When she writes about women's private lives and insists that women should have more knowledge and freedom in determining their domestic, sexual, and reproductive destinies, she comes across as a harbinger of contemporary feminism. When she attacks the suffrage movement and expresses skepticism about the capacity of women for politics and public life, she reads as reactionary. Snyder says it well when she concludes that "within the volatile spheres of feminist and anti-feminist debate, pseudonyms allowed Hastings to experiment in voice and perspective; to change argumentative tack; and, finally, to refuse *all* settled positions."

Hastings also experiments with different voices in her literary work, which spans several different genres. Though *The New Age* is not as well known for poetry as many other magazines of its era, it published poems in most issues, and Hastings contributed poetry regularly. No one would mistake her for a great lost poet, but at her best she is a compelling writer of formal verse. As I argue in my essay later in this book, some of her most interesting writing about the lives of women is in her poems, where she depicts women who openly express sexual desire or defy conventions of gender. Though she is hardly the poetic equal of Edna St. Vincent Millay, she is like Millay in that her traditional formal approach can obscure just how modern she is. Certainly "The Lost Bacchante," in which a priestess of Bacchus appears in a city to spread sexual havoc, is a clever modernization of classical source material.

Hastings also wrote a great deal of fiction, including serialized works and short stories. Due to restrictions of space, this book does not contain much of her serial prose work, but a full study of her fiction would have to consider the Hardy-esque domestic realist drama *Whited Sepulchres* from 1909 and the satirical romance *The Maids' Comedy* from 1910. Hastings published the latter as a stand-alone book in 1911, only to fall victim to a shady publisher who ended up having most copies of the novel pulped to cover his debts.[12] She also wrote several serial texts that skirt the line between memoir and fiction: the aforementioned *Pages from an Unpublished Novel* in 1912, as well as an unpublished French novella from the late 1910's called *Minnie Pinnikin*,[13] and two serial works which appeared in her early 1930's newspaper *The Straight-Thinker: Madame Six* and *The Picnic of the Babe in the Woods*. Tyler Babbie's essay in this book focuses on Hastings's experimental short fiction, which she produced several examples of from 1911 to 1913. In her short story "Post-Impressionism," Hastings represents and in some ways spoofs the English response to the first London art exhibit to focus on Cezanne, Matisse, and Van Gogh. Babbie's reading of the story "Modernism" hinges on just how new the term modernism was in 1911. Hastings's story is one of the first uses of the term in any magazine of the period, and as Babbie points out, it "may be the first published work in English that self-designates as 'modernism.'"

Hastings also took on the role of literary critic throughout her career. She had a long-running anonymous column in *The New Age* titled "Present-Day Criticism" which contained reviews of contemporary literature and the latest editions of rival periodicals. She is at her best when observing the wider literary and political discourse of her time, and even in texts that seem on their face to be personal essays or memoirs, such as "Impressions of Paris" or *Madame Six*, she tends to switch tracks into analysis of contemporary literature, art, and culture. However, her most enduring literary criticism comes in the form of parody. Hastings used her pseudonym T.K.L. for all manner of parody and satire, but she was particularly adept at spoofing writers we now think of as giants of high modernism. "Wake Up, England!" is a spot-on parody of the Futurist manifestos of Marinetti.

In 1913, T.K.L. picked a fascinating fight with Ezra Pound. Hastings's relationship to Pound was complicated: she claims to have been responsible for overcoming Orage's objections to ensure that Pound was a regular *New Age* contributor,[14] but she also wrote in "Impressions of Paris" that "the state of things in Art which Mr. Pound deplores is somewhat due to just such florid, pedantic, obscurantist critics as himself—Ixions whom not even an introduction to the almighty gods can clear of pretension."[15] Hastings's feelings about Pound exemplify her feelings about the avant-garde in general: she was clearly receptive to new developments in the arts, as can be seen in her own experimental writing or her championing of Modigliani, but she was also quite willing to mock what she saw as obscurity for the sake of obscurity. She brought this latter tendency to the fore when Pound began writing a series of seven *New Age* essays about contemporary poetry in September 1913. Two weeks into his series, Hastings, in her T.K.L. guise, began writing parodies of Pound's essays that appeared in the same issues as his ongoing series. Often their essays were just a page or two apart from each other. Sunny Stalter-Pace's essay in this book spells out just how specific Hastings could be in spoofing Pound's bombastic self-assuredness. Stalter-Pace also explores a more serious argument about avant-garde poetics that is threaded through the T.K.L. parodies, with Hastings speaking up for "the English literary tradition that Pound dismisses wholesale."

In 1914, Hastings left England for Paris and entered a new phase of her career. Her romantic relationship with Orage had long-since waned, as had a brief dalliance with Wyndham Lewis. Hastings ceased her editing duties for *The New Age* at this point, but she continued writing for the paper, primarily under the pseudonym Alice Morning. Celia Kingsbury's essay in this book deals with this phase of Hastings's career, when she settled in Montparnasse, moved in social circles with the likes of Picasso and Max Jacob, reported back to England on daily life in Paris at the start of the First World War, and became Modigliani's lover, model, and financial safety net. For obvious reasons, many of the stories about Hastings from this period feel apocryphal or exaggerated, not least because Modigliani and Hastings had several domestic violence incidents that were much-gossiped-about.[16] Kingsbury's essay explores the ways that Hastings both participated in and resisted this myth-making in her weekly essay series "Impressions of Paris," which appeared in *The New Age* throughout 1914 and 1915. Seven of the "Impressions" are included in this book, and they are, as Scholes argues, "lively, accomplished prose, as good as any journalism written at that time."[17] To the extent that Hastings is known today, it is probably as Modigliani's model. (She was his second-most-frequent portrait sitter.)[18] But the "Impressions" demonstrate that Hastings was an artist in her own right in her Paris years: witty, observant, occasionally furious, humiliated but never defeated, and devoted to capturing the spirit of a city in perilous times.

Hastings remained in Paris for the rest of the decade, and after her relationship with Modigliani faded, she became involved with the young French novelist Raymond Radiguet. She worked on the surrealist novella *Minnie Pinnikin,* though it was never published, and the frequency of her *New Age* contributions declined. In 1920, she was hospitalized with what she called a "fibrous excrescence" (probably uterine fibroids) and underwent surgery.[19] In shapshots of herself dated 1918 and 1924, Hastings uses the same caption—"very ill." She published no significant work in the twenties, and spent much of her time in Switzerland and the French provinces convalescing.[20]

By 1932, she was back in England, and looking to get back into the literary world. She edited the short-lived periodical *The Straight-Thinker,* and used it to publish some of her writing from the intervening years. Most notably, she published *Madame Six,* a serial account of her time in the hospital awaiting surgery. Two installments of *Madame Six* are included in this book. Its style is in some respects a continuation of the style of "Impressions of Paris"—observations about her daily life interspersed with cultural criticism—except that her daily life is limited to a hospital ward. In the thirties, she also deepened her interest in theosophy and published several books on the subject, including a lengthy defense of Theosophical Society founder Madame Helena Blavatsky. She struck up correspondences with theosophists in Canada, and most of what little survives of her correspondence and photographs, including the photographs in this book, is housed in the Helena P. Blavatsky Library in Toronto.

Theosophy was Hastings's major interest in her later years, but her secondary interest was reclaiming and defending her own career. *Madame Six* frequently comments on the literary scene of the 1910's, but her longest retrospective work is *The Old "New Age": Orage and Others*, which appeared in a small edition in 1936. Hastings wrote the book to call attention to her contributions to *The New Age* and correct what she believed were exaggerations of Orage's importance in retrospective accounts of the magazine. The book is undoubtedly spiteful—it takes her all of three pages to compare Orage to Hitler and Mussolini—and while John Carswell's description of it being "written in a fury of jealousy and literary depravation" reads as dismissive and even misogynistic,[21] he is not wrong that the book combines venomous anti-Orage invective with disbelief at her own obscurity. If not for *The Old "New Age,"* we likely would not know the full scope of Hastings's writing—it is the only place where she ever laid claim to all of her pseudonyms. We also would not have this marvelously defiant description of herself:

> Whoever may have changed from the early days, I have not. I am still the author of "Woman's Worst Enemy, Woman", as well as of "The Maids' Comedy"; I still love the social rebel, and challenge mere man-made laws and hate the Pankhursts, Emmeline and Christabel, who sold the Feminist movement; I am the same crusading, anti-philistine woman I ever was.[22]

Hastings committed suicide in 1943 after a long illness. Even as so many of the people she had loved or battled—or both—were being enshrined as the central literary and historical figures of the century, she was forgotten. Inevitably with a writer like this, one begins asking why her work so faded from view, and there are a number of answers. Most obviously, her use of pseudonyms makes it difficult to gain a sense of the scope of her work if one does not already know what to look for. I personally discovered Hastings when I stumbled upon the T.K.L. essay "All Against Anything" while doing research on the French poet and previous Unsung Masters Series subject Francis Jammes. I thought T.K.L. was hilarious, but it took me a fair amount of digging to figure out who she was (and to figure out that she was a she) even with Google, the MLA Bibliography, and the Modernist Journals Project website at my disposal. Hastings's play with pseudonyms makes her a fascinating writer, but it has also meant that for most of the past century the breadth of her oeuvre has been invisible to all but the most narrowly focused scholars.

Her legacy is also difficult to label. Read her early poems ("Vashti" and "The Lost Bacchante" especially) or the opening pages of her book *Woman's Worst Enemy: Woman*, and you might think that you have stumbled upon a proto-third-wave feminist visionary, but then you read on into her anti-suffragette essays as D. Triformis and she comes across as borderline misogynist. "Feminist," then, is not a fitting label. She wrote tricky experimental fiction; her pseudonyms destabilized the idea of a unified authorial voice; she printed early work by Pound, Flint, and Mansfield in her role as *New Age* literary editor; as a critic she was skeptical of realist fiction; and her list of romantic entanglements is a who's who of European modernism. So "modernist" starts to seem like it might be a fair label. However, she was an astonishingly effective parodist and critic of new trends in art, and repeatedly expressed distaste for free verse poetics. She would be easier to promote if she were simply a forgotten modernist innovator or a lost feminist heroine, but she was neither. To be sure, reading Hastings deepens our understanding of the history of both modernism and feminism, but that deepening comes from the ways she resisted these emerging discourses even as she keenly understood them.

She also cannot be defined by a commitment to a particular genre—this book contains political essays, parodies, short fiction, memoir, and poetry, and if we had another hundred pages we might delve into her novels, literary criticism, or spiritualist writing as well. Our series title Unsung Masters makes an implicit claim for each of the featured authors, but it might be more accurate to say in the case of Hastings that she was a jack of all genres, and perhaps a master of none. She was, however, a master of the periodical. In the weekly give-and-take of *The New Age*, she found the perfect outlet for her brash, roaming intellect. Due to the excellent work of the Modernist Journals Project, the full run of *The New Age* is available online, and I would encourage anyone interested in grappling with the full scope of Hastings's career to visit their website. Her best writing in any genre is very much of its moment—she shines when attacking an article published in a rival magazine a week earlier, or describing the immediate Parisian reaction to news stories that would be forgotten a year later, or in parodying a social event from the day before. This sort of writing can be powerfully, palpably alive, but timeliness is often the enemy of timelessness, and as Hastings herself once wrote, "one doesn't write Impressions with an eye on Immortality."[23] Still, even if she is not immortal, she nevertheless should be remembered as more than Modigliani's model or Orage's spiteful ex-lover. Her best writing is exciting, funny, and a bit discomfiting, and it offers a unique perspective on some of the key historical and literary moments of the twentieth century.

-BJ

NOTES

1. Stephen Gray, *Beatrice Hastings: A Literary Life* (New York: Penguin, 2004), 41.

2. According to WorldCat, only 33 copies of the book exist in libraries around the world. There are currently no copies for sale on Amazon in any format. That said, if you want to do any sort of serious study of Hastings's work, the book is a must-read.

3. Gray, 94-104.

4. Ibid., 108.

5. Book V of *Pages from an Unpublished Novel*, not included in this book, also narrates the death of an infant. It was published in *The New Age* on July 25, 1912.

6. Beatrice Hastings, *The Old "New Age": Orage and Others* (London: Blue Moon Press, 1936), 19.

7. Gray, 143.

8. Ibid., 206-9.

9. Hastings, *The Old "New Age,"* 43.

10. Ibid., 7-8.

11. Another interesting exchange not included in this book is in *The New Age* on October 17, 1912, where Hastings uses her anonymous column "Present-Day Criticism" to criticize the poem "Ariadne in Nysa" by Beatrice Hastings, which had appeared in *The New Age* on May 9, 1912.

12. Gray, 217.

13. Portions of *Minnie Pinnikin* have been translated into English and published in Kenneth Wayne's *Modigliani and the Artists of Montparnasse* (New York: Harry N. Abrams, 2002). The original French manuscript is at the Museum of Modern Art in New York.

14. Hastings, *The Old "New Age,"* 6-7.

15. Alice Morning (Beatrice Hastings), "Impressions of Paris," *The New Age*, January 21, 1915, 309.

16. Gray, 414-5.

17. Robert Scholes, *Parodoxy of Modernism* (New Haven: Yale University Press, 2006), 226.

18. Gray, 315.

19. Beatrice Hastings, "*Madame Six*: Part II," *The Straight-Thinker*, February 6, 1932, 15.

20. Hastings, *The Old "New Age,"* 29.

21. John Carswell, *Lives and Letters* (New York: New Directions, 1978), 224.

22. Hastings, *The Old "New Age,"* 9.

23. Alice Morning (Beatrice Hastings), "Impressions of Paris," *The New Age*, July 22, 1915, 277.

POLITICAL ESSAYS

WOMAN'S WORST ENEMY: WOMAN

Beatrice Tina

In 1909, The New Age Press printed a small book by Beatrice Tina called Woman's Worst Enemy: Woman. *The book consists of seven essays, including a slightly rewritten version of the essay "Woman as State Creditor," which had appeared in* The New Age *on June 27, 1908 as a response to E. Belfort Bax's "Feminism and Female Suffrage," a two-part essay which had appeared in* The New Age *on May 30 and June 13. Bax had argued that, contrary to arguments of the suffrage movement, women in fact are a "privileged order of human beings" due to legal rights they have against men. Tina's essay, and eventually her book, responds to Bax, but also branches out into a much wider consideration of how societal assumptions about maternity, sex, and gender roles shape the lives of women.*

DECLARATORY

A MONG all the employments of human life which offer themselves to my choice, I should certainly never have selected that of maternity. Never, at any time of my whole existence, did I want to become a mother. As a very young girl the knowledge of the process shocked and repelled me, and I could never hear a reference to birth without experiencing nausea. Among visions of beauty and delight I dwelled in my inner mind until the rude shock of knowledge showed me a yawning pit of human pain; and this abyss, I was told, was the way all women had to go.

I determined, in a spirit of royal freedom, that I would not go that way; but ignorance overthrew me and so it comes that the ugly mystery of birth, veiled by distrusting woman from the eyes of beauty-adoring man, is illumined by me with no borrowed lamp, but with the flame of my own well-to-be-forgotten memories.

This book is written for the pleasure of denouncing the sort of female whose modesty howls for silence on such important matters as sex and maternity. She tells her daughters that they grew in cabbages or were brought by the doctor, concealing her own sexuality thereby. When the girls grow to maidenhood she has another set of lies ready, and a veil and orange blossoms, and any amount of temporary congratulation, so that they may go quietly to the altar and be made even as she herself before they discover her deception. Truly, they might not go quietly if they knew what was before them.

To some strange man is usually entrusted the task of shocking a young girl's modesty and fierce pride of virginity, at the risk of her rebellion against the astounding situation of the marriage-night.

It is safe to say, that almost no English girl is ever allowed, let alone forced, to witness a birth before entering herself upon maternity. Too delicate, too sensitive, this victimised creature, to witness what it must be her portion to experience! Hypocrisy can no deeper hide than in this iniquitous sentiment.

———◆———

It is difficult for one who has suffered the soiling of a promising life through the wicked conspiracy against youth, to remember that much of this conspiracy is carried on by persons less guilty of sin than folly. But it is small consolation to me that my persecutors knew not what they did! Nor do I pray forgiveness for them until they turn from their ways.

I bear the stigma on my soul of an unwilling maternity. Not from any fault of mine. Never did I contemplate committing this horrible crime against a future human being. Not for the smile of my family or of society, not to give any man a son or daughter, not to gain anything whatsoever of all earth's possessions, would I have consented.

———◆———

The pain and degradation of unwilling maternity destroyed for ever that barrier of golden illusion which had always stood between my soul and the vulgar horrors of human existence. If any one says in the cant of orthodoxy that it was for my good that I learned to know the reality of life and pain, I reply that, knowing it the more, I wish I had been left with my illusion. All who wish it are welcome to their experiences of pain. The difference between them and the being who is free from pain is the difference between devils and angels; and the difference between devils and humans is the cant vanity: "We suffer to grow good!"

It has been asserted to me that young girls discuss sex and maternity and are by no means ignorant of the facts. None of my young companions, with one exception, ever talked of these things. The exception was a girl who told my astounded and horrified innocence that a newly-married woman had advised her to have all her children as quickly as possible, so as to get it all over at once: you had to have your number! I remember the feeling of disgust I experienced for an instant, and the flame of revolt which shot through me; and I said that I did not want any children at all; and my young friend replied that she would like to have two "to dress up." [1]

———◆———

At home, I never heard but once any word except the usual biblicalised platitudes about marriage and olive branches. One day my mother was seized with internal cramp. There was no one but myself in the house with her, and I applied hot flannels and massage according to her direction. When she was somewhat relieved, I ventured a question which had suggested itself to me: Is childbirth like this? And in her pain she stared at me and told me the truth. "Oh, poor girl!" she exclaimed, "this is nothing to be compared with that."

It is not the way of youth to dwell upon miserable facts. In my search for delight and beauty, I forgot my mother's confession. Indeed, I believe no warning or description of the deliveries of women might have profited me much, for youth is selfish, and I was confident that I should have no children. I did not know to

———

[1] Hastings also uses this anecdote in her serialized *Pages from an Unpublished Novel* on July 11, 1912.

what extent human beings are enslaved, or that one's will is liable to be betrayed by the flesh, *unless the mind is fully informed.* If I had been educated in that which I had a right to know—the imminent development of sex impulse and the scientific prevention of conception, I would have been spared much bewilderment of soul and the black atheism which denies any good at all, but sees in the very delights of love only an inexcusable deception. The simple truth that maternity, like fighting, exploring, &c., need only be followed by those who choose, would have left me free to behold dignity in both God and Woman, whom I was forced to declaim Tyrant and Victim. Men I grew to regard as merely the callous instruments of the cruelty.

Priests declare that it is a law that maternity must result from woman's participation in the pleasure of sex. But it is none the less a fact that science has discovered many simple devices for abrogating this law. The result of men's cruel suppression of these discoveries is that, with increasing aversion from maternity, numberless women continue to bear unwanted children, to whom they bequeath a failing generative energy, which finally weakens the whole nation into sterility and ignominious decay. Men seem to ignore the fact that they are born of women, and may inherit an unwilling mother's disgust of living.

A decadent nation, in attempting to restore its energy by forcing women into becoming mothers, merely burns the candle at both ends. There is only one possible way in which such a State may recuperate its strength, and that way is to imitate the instinct of young nations in neglecting marriage bonds and giving its women sex-liberty, so that those with the strongest maternal instinct may freely direct the genius of motherhood. But a decadent nation is a nation bound by every fetter of property and title, and the day of each generation being short, individual greed prevents any relaxing of legislation until the day when some invading enemy arrives, and the remnant of one more power goes into slavery.

It is a significant fact about England that while free love is too common to evoke an adjective, the cant about the sanctity of marriage forbids that any breach of this law should be "found out"—that is, should result in a child—under penalty of disgrace.

A German artist who ruined his poetry by interpolating philosophical misinformation, wrote: "Man wants to live! woman only wants to be the means to his life." The history of all civilisation gives the lie to this bumptious masculinism. Civilised woman wants something more than to be the means to man's life: she wants to live herself. It is man's stupid denial of her right to live her own life which sends his civilisations toppling.

I so hated at one time being female that I could have denied the fact. But with increasing disrespect for and criticism of the home-made fetish man the superior, and with subsequent reflection upon the position of woman as the enemy and man as the ignominious decoy of nature, I realised and was mollified to perceive that the duel in the last resort is between woman and nature; and, judging from the census returns, it is warrantable to lay the odds on woman.

I have sometimes said to elderly women who sought to convince me that in maternity a woman found her highest joy: "Pray set aside, then, a class of women to bear the children; I and my class don't want to;" and very surely has come the objection: "It is not fair that some should bear all the burden, and others go off to enjoy themselves." The conclusion I have drawn from this is that these foolish women deliberately lied about the pure joy, &c. But like the fox, who had cut off his tail, and the sick who would fain see every one sick, these resentful and malicious creatures endeavour to drag all women into the dull pit of their disappointing experience. Worse, they borrow and quote for their own purpose the gospel of the perfect mother who suffers nothing in delivering a child.

To the perfect mother the whole process of maternity should be from beginning to end a sensuous and a spiritual enjoyment. I understand that there are still such women extant. Less inconvenienced by an accouchement than by a visit to the dentist, the mild pangs of their labour compared with those of most women are as the ripples of a lake to the crashing breakers which tear a vessel asunder. Best-born of a nation are the children of such mothers. Yet no especial honour of upbringing is accorded these children; no money is spent to insure that the heritage of graces naturally bestowed by so nearly divine parturition shall be increased. Nay! all the money to spare goes in building hospitals for healing the uterine diseases of women whose maternity is a crime, and in prisons, asylums, and hydropathics for their luckless progeny.

————◆————

To my youthful disgust at the idea of childbirth I add a conclusion. Never have I seen the adult creature of whom I would like to be the mother.

THE THREE SISTERS

THE PROFESSIONAL WOMAN—THE WIFE—THE ARTISAN

SINCE THE DAYS when men sorely needed sons to lighten labour, the necessity of the wife has stultified the rise of woman. Man subjected woman as wife, and the barren wife and the unwed woman were enslaved by the mother of children. Scorn and spite were poured upon the childless from the days of Leah to the days of our grandmothers, when the professional woman and the spinster revolted against the tyranny of the breeder.

————◆————

The wife has gained for all women our epithets of tyrant, and the like. Her hands sent forth Hagar into the wilderness as to-day her rules condemn unmarried mothers and their helpless offspring. Men do not condemn Hagar, but, for dread of their women's accusations, they dare do nothing, bullied and blackmailed into cruelty and cowardice.

For the maintenance of her supreme position over the rest of her sex, the wife has demanded the persecution of her unmarried sisters. In the books of the last century is many a vivid glimpse of the degradation from which the single woman has uprisen. Spite and contumely were her portion. The single woman was a butt.

———◆———

It is interesting to note the way in which the wife has subjected man also.

A man's position in society is only less valuable than his life, and yet this position is dependent upon women's conventions.

It scarcely needs proving that a member of any public body retains his office mainly through his subjection to the rules of the bed-and-board women. No minister could survive an action for restitution of conjugal rights.

The wife must be for ever kept and clothed, bedded and paraded. And with the parading goes the lip-homage she loves. Wonder is it none that philosophers execrate both women and marriage.

———◆———

A note on this lip-homage.

Of all the millions of money expended by the State of England, not one farthing is voted for the aid of mothers. If the husband can support his wife, well and good; but if the woman be left a widow, even though she be pregnant, she must depend upon the charity of her relations or the workhouse. There is no human creature more word worshipped or more contemptuously neglected. Madonna-worship is the cheapest of all.

———◆———

The fault is at her own door. She has been satisfied and puffed up with word-worship. She has sacrificed man, woman, and child upon her altar.

Selfish, vain, and credulous creature! whose sins rebound with so terrible directness. Yet while her folly goes unrestrained, how canker-like is its effect! Men must give up their freedom who accept her inexorable terms. Women who are not of her order suffer insolence and the pushing of her hands. And the children! What thanks should they give the poor-spirited thing who dares to bear them, with not the qualification a man would demand who bred a dog for a show; who hurls into life unfortunate heirs of her stunted intelligence, her narrow hips, and her quailing womb—all sooner than remain unmarried—all sooner than take her chance of competition in the world?

Yet from these children, she demands thanks. From the cradle she rears them to worship her. They grow, and they come to suspect her. They leave the home at the earliest moment. But the old, bad hypnotism clings; the cripple, the criminal, the consumptive, scarcely dare curse his mother.

———— ♦ ————

But at length men are beginning to recognise that the wife is not so urgent a necessity. The lip-homage, never paid to the wife as woman, but as mother, is less frequent than of yore, since machinery yearly reduces the value of her output.

So far it is still economically cheaper to breed labour from women than to make machinery. But time passes. The inventions of men multiply. And the wife must awake to learn what economic values mean, and to understand that the products of her throes have hitherto been indispensable as the cheapest of all labour.

The wife vilifies the professional women who do understand these economic values, and who see in the disgust and horror with which men who know only domestic women regard their enfranchisement, a real horror and a real disgust only to be assuaged by the presentation of a new type of woman, efficient and intellectualised.

———— ♦ ————

Among the names of wives handed down by history, few are more belauded than those of Sarah, Andromache, and Cornelia. Sarah, the tyrant, pitiless, vain, and a murderess at heart! Andromache, the feeble, whining slave who gave her little son to death with scarce a struggle. Weak and narrow-brained wife and mother, contemptible concubine to her husband's murderer, her true quality has been hidden behind her vanity in the glory of Hector's name.

And for Cornelia—who may paint this furious and ambitious matron? Vanity could not deeper lurk than in the bosom of this Roman woman, igniting a gossip by that exhibition of her ill-starred children, her "jewels."

————•————

The third of the sisters, the woman artisan, was formerly the mental drudge of the wife. She too has evolved, however, and to-day she is found in the factories and the smaller commercial businesses.

Before she rebelled and threw off the slavery to which the once all-powerful wife subjected her, mistresses of households might have a dozen drudges in as many years to wear out for little more than barest keep. Now the poorer woman has changed all that. She refuses to hire herself for domestic service; and the wife, unwilling to do the work, moves into a tiny hutch with her tethered mate, and even then finds an occasional charwoman indispensable. The respectable sums demanded by these temporary helps, and their independent manners, have gained for them a status never conceded to the bygone family slave, so irresistibly sobriquetted "the slavey."

The wife, reflecting her husband's value, with her silver tea-service manners and a dozen gossips to pass the afternoon away, must soon pay her servants not merely in money but in honours as well. The mistress is beginning to realise that the willing drudge is extinct; and well she knows who is the real mistress if by chance a capable maidservant enters her villa.

————•————

Idle, vain, and self-distrustful wife-woman, aspirant in some ancient era to indulgences never enjoyed save in name only, your unforeseeing greed has too long doomed the whole race of women. Who would pity you? Yet, who might refrain from pitying? For as man's intellect invents civilisation and refining measures for himself, he begets your bodies finer, and your agonies in labour increase with every increase of his comfort.

Yet you must be dumb, since to avow your aversion from maternity is to lose all that you have been able to proclaim as your distinction from harlots and slaves—the title of wife and child-bearer.

If you refuse to be a wife, what else may you be?

Shut within the jealous walls of your home, what means have you of acquiring knowledge of life, the which might make you as little afraid of risking your existence in the world as man himself? Your sisters who have so risked existence live upon such honourable and respected terms among men as you, choked under your worn titles, are unable to imagine.

It is your choice to expect men to support you—father, husband, or relation; and when these fail you with charity you are content.

Incompetent! cunning doll before marriage, tyrant as soon as the novelty has tarnished, retaliation is overtaking you.

Denunciation of your crimes against the Soul of Woman is almost silenced in contemplating your unenviable and degrading future, from which each one of all your class—O deluded! believes she, at least, may escape.

WOMAN AS STATE CREDITOR

TO THE PEDDLING catalogue of legal advantages said to be enjoyed by a few women law-breakers, I attach a disability which women suffer, and only by their suffering of which Law and Man have become Law and Man: I mean, of course, the endurance of maternity. The enormity of this disability makes that catalogue as trivial an honour to women as the signature of a tourist to a pyramid. The preferences, denounced so deliriously, are indeed the Law's way of saying to women: "I'm proud to know you." But they do not help us in the least.

No man-made laws, no man-given preferences, can really help women. Women alone know what women need. If it is true that women are permitted to tell lies in court "with impunity"; if a woman can claim support from a man she has voluntarily deserted; if a wife can beat her husband whenever she likes: I reply that I, personally, am ungrateful for my privileges.

I, and all women, want things much more important than the privilege of lying; things no man can have any conception of unless he realises that women love liberty of mind and body as much as himself.

But this love of liberty is the very sentiment the anti-feminist denies as integral in Woman. The denial is part of the familiar, ignorant argument: "Women do not realise, let alone dislike, their enslavement." Certainly there are still women whose release from the harem seems to be halting: whose attitude savours of the seraglio; who stand shivering within the friendly threshold of the modern Pasha, dreading the step outward. These women count. They will be the tail of the snake, wriggling long after the beast has been dispatched. But they are reckoned with already. It is not inconceivable that the term "wife" may become opprobrious. The position of kept wife will be generally held—as it is to-day by thousands of English spinsters—to be degrading; only women of dull capacity and sensual habits will be found permanently living on men.

The anti-feminist's tirade against the State which "privileges" married women, is therefore belated. The Law, in this matter, is, for once, not a "hass." However tardily, however clumsily, it stands deciding that the State has a tacit bargain with the women who accept the disability of marriage and maternity. But the whole mess of "fatuously-generous" repayments, listed as "privileges," is not a bit of use to us; and, since we have said so, the continued proffer of them strikes us as being insulting and contemptuous. The return made for women's disability in bearing children is meanly inadequate.

Exactly how this disability affects women, and how to relieve the most distressing pressure of it, only women can understand. And on this ground alone the whole pretension of a man-run State may be proved indefensible.

It has long been the practice among women to conspire to lie about maternity. The torture of childbirth is the ugliest fact in human life. Women instinctively veil its horrors from that sensitive creature, the husband. He is narcotised, englamoured, wrapped in cottonwool, and sent a message that he may not be upset by his wife's cries. There is just a shadow of excuse for the callousness of family men who are deceived in these ways. But is it because of ignorance that, although women constantly die in childbirth, there is yet no legislation on the matter? Is it from ignorance that Father Vaughan is belauded who, with vile language, would whip women into the ordeal although every nerve in their system warns them not to attempt maternity? Is it from ignorance that any man who supports a mother-woman subjects her to this ordeal year after year, in health and out of health, just as long as the poor thing can endure it and live? Is it from ignorance that such a man is not brought to book?

We are loth to grant the excuse of ignorance, but if we must grant it, we order: "Move aside, and let women who understand women see to this thing!" A woman's parliament will very soon ordain that no pregnant woman be left to the mercy of her ignorant husband any more than a child is now left to the mercy of its ignorant parents.

I saw a friend recently who was awaiting delivery. There were two unmarried women and myself with her. One of these, her sister, told me in an astonished aside that "'T.' didn't seem to mind." The girls went out for a cycle ride. Immediately "T." looked at me piteously and then out over the sunshiny fields, and she said: "I have never had a summer free since I was married. I almost wish I could die this time!"

The natural depression of a pregnant woman? Just so. And no wonder that the most intelligent of single women, piercing the veil which the wife wraps around her mortification, consign husbands and their consequences to the limbo of over-rated things.

Few men are permitted to pierce this veil. The anti-feminist has not pierced it. That is why he denounces so loudly the women who prefer interests and take up work outside marriage. The housewife says little; the house-husband says much. He says, like Dickens's drunken baron: "My wife is no worse off than other men's wives." Nay, the anti-feminist says more: "Other women shall not be better off than my wife."

Women will not cry to dull ears the facts about pregnancy. Among themselves each one, up to the measure of her own suffering—and to that measure only—understands. To a highly-developed, imaginative woman maternity means months of odious ignominy, and finally a struggle with death as through waves of flame. And no alleviative surgery ever discovered is worth the adjective. Everybody in this scientific time can point to some man he knows whose wife has died in childbirth. Civilisations go down successively before this failure to abrogate the curse upon Eve.

The comparison is often made of the risks of a soldier's life with those of maternity. Medea stated her sentiments on the subject some time ago. Of course there is no parallel. As soldiers men run risks, it is true, when on active service; but they are risks only. Moreover, they have an element of adventure, and are stimulating and often enjoyable. Maternity is neither adventurous, stimulating, nor enjoyable; nor merely a risk. Its horrors are certain, and the oppression of their slow and sure approach is unrelieved by a single chance of escape, save death.

It is clear to women that the first feeble attempt to recompense them for their share in the making of humanity, is based on a callous repudiation of the magnitude of their service; and I repeat that even the shoddy return proffered is worthless because misdirected.

Naive and childlike man has determined the contract both for himself and for us. But he has exhausted our innocence. We are prepared to draw up our own terms now; and the fiercer the opposition, the more certain we become of the extent of man's addiction to tyranny.

The militant suffragettes have saved us from the last ignominy of the slave—the obligation to give thanks for enfranchisement.

FROM REPLIES TO CORRESPONDENTS

"*A MERE ORDINARY MAN.*"—"To-day, unlike their grandmothers, women are free to die maids unpersecuted, if so they will."

True! True, also, you belong to the party who would shut them off from all but domestic service. You say, "The fates forbid universal suffrage: since a mere ordinary man like myself will come badly off on that threatened day when women will have power in the land."

"*A MOTHER IN ISRAEL.*"—You are "surprised and saddened" at me? The birth of each of your children has meant "toil and struggle, relinquishing of cherished interests and ambitions," yet you consider you "have fulfilled your highest destiny." Possibly; yet a little more self-education, a little more time to know yourself, a few interests outside your narrow circle of childbirth, toil, and struggle might have made you think differently. These are bitter words of yours: "At present the shame of motherhood lies in the fact that it is in almost every case compulsory, and not voluntary." I presume you mean me to infer other women's motherhood, not yours. You seem fairly well acquainted with the facts which you are "surprised and saddened" to hear me mention.

"*A WIFE.*"—"Let me tell Beatrice Tina that a wife who loves her husband is glad to suffer for him."

This masochist sort of self-abasement does not seem commendable to me. Am I to understand conversely that the husband is glad to have this wife suffer for him? No wonder there are so many perverts in England.

"A MARRIED MAN."—"'The torture of childbirth' is quite an erroneous expression. 'Every nerve in some women's bodies warn them not to attempt maternity.' Their nerves do nothing of the sort; quite the reverse. Anyway, woman, by nature more inclined sexually, is the guilty party. We are told of the ignominy of being in the family way. It is a time replete with glorious possibilities."

Yes; one might produce this historian of the mother-feeling.

ANOTHER MAN.—"Women have been known to have felt no pain at that period. These suffragettes are undoubtedly man-haters. They love to dream of the time when men shall be amenable to the rules laid down by these tyrants—even to the extent of self-negation...Let all true women march with us to our mutual emancipation, and then we shall be able to show our chivalry and true love."

We don't want your chivalry. It has meant to us that we have been deluded into being amenable to the laws laid down by men—"even to the extent of self-negation." But we, for our part, have no intention of mocking men with "chivalry."

AND A SORT OF WOMAN.—"My own experience was of an hour's hard muscular exercise. I would prefer it to an afternoon with the dentist. Of course, one meets women who have suffered horribly, but this may be the merest chance...Never shall I forget the description given by a man who had had a tooth out, the same man who had inflicted yearly motherhood upon his wife. His own daughter, the eldest of eleven, told me she loathed the very word 'birthday.'"

The most astounding revelation I have received through these letters is the light indifference with which happy mothers relate and dismiss the sufferings of the less fortunate. In the face of the sad woman's story she tells, this writer concludes that maternity is "from beginning to end adventurous, stimulating, and enjoyable." For her, it happens to be, and except for the selfish coldness of her sentence, "Of course, one meets women who have suffered, but this may be the merest chance," one would say that here was the ideal mother person. But three pages of detailed chatter about other women's miseries make me fear that here, indeed, is merely one of the gossipping, dull, and insensitive females, from whom we need not expect the broad sympathy which is as inseparable a quality of the true mother as swift and painless labour.

"*E.B.*"—"There are many unhappy marriages…but tender devotion is often shown by a husband towards his expectant wife."

An admission, forsooth! We are to suppose again that the neglected ones do not matter.

"*LLWYD AP GWLYN.*"—"Beatrice Tina! take care, for they who do not understand are legion. You are showing a little of your woman's heart. Hide it, or vultures will tear it."

Vultures never venture to touch a living heart. What should I fear, whom the malign experiences of modern social existence have been powerless to enslave?

THE FAILURE OF MILITANCY

D. Triformis[1]

The New Age, January 20, 1910

THE LEADERS proceed along their narrow bureaucratic path, urging more violence. Miss Christabel Pankhurst, in an article entitled bravely, "Powder and Shot for the Campaign," in the last issue of "Votes for Women," compares the protest of men against women's violence with their own conduct when appealing against injustice.[2] She writes: "The militant methods of the W.S.P.U. are sometimes severely condemned by men who express strong disapproval of unlawful or violent action. It is edifying, therefore, to notice how quick are these same men critics when temptation comes to them to adopt militant methods themselves." Either that paragraph is an apology for or a justification of women's violence. Apology never having been part of the W.S.P.U. attitude, we accept the alternative, and

---

[1] D. Triformis was a pseudonym Hastings used to write essays attacking the suffrage movement, and in particular the Woman's Social and Political Union under the leadership of co-founders Emmeline and Christabel Pankhurst. Hastings wrote 17 essays as D. Triformis, all in 1910 and 1911.

[2] Pankhurst's article appeared in the January 14, 1910 issue of *Votes for Women*.

consider the remark as meant to justify women's violence. We must first translate the sarcasm of the term "edifying"; it is surely intended as satire: we should read it as "unedifying." For there can be nothing really edifying, that is, spiritually strengthening, comforting, improving, in the spectacle of men, who in their calmer mood deprecate violence, being carried in a moment of temptation beyond sanity and the ways of peace. As a justification of women's violence, the passionate deeds of men done under temptation take an aspect the reverse of justifying, and constitute a strong condemnation.

In the same number of the W.S.P.U. organ there occurs an expression of censure upon the methods of the Women's Freedom League for the action of some of the members of that League in destroying the ballot-papers. With a rectitude which very nearly cries for a pat on the shoulder, the Pot calls the Kettle black. But where is the precise spot of difference between slapping the face of a police inspector and pouring hair-oil upon ballot-papers? Both actions were done in the way of protest against disenfranchisement. Both were violent and unlawful. Both might be thus justified and thus condemned. We mention the instances to point a conclusion that the W.S.P.U. leaders seem to think that violence should stop somewhere. We ask: Where should it stop? The Freedom League stop at slapping faces; the W.S.P.U. at injuring ballot-papers. Both ballot-papers and police inspectors are in the service of the male electorate. Presumably the W.S.P.U., which, as "Votes for Women" says, "is appealing from the misdeeds of the Government to the good sense of the electors themselves," believes that the electors' good sense may be quicker aroused and their prejudice against woman's franchise deeper allayed, by slaps and brickbats than by putting them to the expense and trouble of a fresh ballot. We do not presume to decide. Our object, in the despair of inducing the W.S.P.U. leaders to discourage violence altogether and to apply once more to reason, is to discover exactly to what extremities of violence they are prepared to go. If the vote is to be won by violence, it must be won by a violence exceeding that which the opponents of women's suffrage are prepared to employ. What indication have we that the leaders of woman's violence will exceed the violence of men and finally conquer by militant methods? True, none of the leaders have been forcibly fed, or frog-marched, or even played upon with a hosepipe. They have, perhaps, not the personal impulse for a terrific retaliation which may justly be supposed to burn in the hearts of the minor members of the Union who have been so outraged. But we cannot thus separate from the interests of the outraged members the leaders who urged these members to pursue the tactics which resulted in imprisonment and torture. There is nothing truly militant in urging persons to conduct involving spiritual degradation and physical agony and then, by way of avenging the loyal sufferers, merely paying out money for an action at common law against those who inflicted the suffering. We are driven to wonder whether, when Mrs. Pankhurst leads the next deputation to Westminster, she will consider a slap on some policeman's face sufficient protest against the injuries her devoted followers have endured.

If by militant tactics the leaders of the W.S.P.U. mean just slaps and an occasional slate or stone thrown "without intention of hurting anyone," as Mr. Gordon Hewart stated in his defence of Miss Davison;[3] if these pin-pricks are all the deeds the militant leaders are prepared for—we can feel no great and overwhelming assurance that the methods will win the vote. The women are employing slaps as weapons against men who do not hesitate to

---

[3] W.S.P.U. member Emily Davison was arrested for throwing stones through the window of a Liberal Party club. When she barricaded her cell door in Strangeways Prison, prison officials attempted to use a hose to flood her cell and force her out, though they were eventually able to break down the door. Sir Gordon Hewart, who later became Lord Chief Justice of England and Wales, was Davison's plaintiff's attorney when she sued for damages.

reply with a hose-pipe. There can be small doubt as to which side will win in such an unequal combat. The greater force must prevail in a battle waged by force.

This question of the suffrage will never be settled by force, for the reason that the women are less certain of the utility of force than the evil and backward men who have control of the prisons. Three years of urging the members of the W.S.P.U. to militant methods has only produced amongst the most doughty an impulse to fling a stone or a ginger-beer bottle, "without intent to injure anyone." Clearly, the women do not want to use force. Even after they have suffered appalling indignities and risked permanent injury to themselves under the hands of jailers and prison doctors, they do not become the prey of their passions. They are then even more disposed to refrain from a violence similar to that which, when exhibited by low and coarse officials, fills the women with spiritual concern, though not with bodily fear. It is impossible for such women not to understand that the standard of woman's suffrage, seized by violence, would be a standard seized in the dark, and poisoned, perchance, by blood whose bane might transform the triumph into consuming bitterness.

The leaders of the W.S.P.U. have clamoured for militancy. The W.S.P.U. has not responded. Civilisation holds firm its place in the minds of women. An attempt to defend themselves from the degenerate lads employed as stewards—an attempt which might, unblamed, have resorted to extreme measures: a few stones and empty bottles—that is about all one may produce as progeny of the historic slap. Petty riot and petty damage committed by a handful of persons; by the majority of those belonging to the Union—no riot, no damage, but a steady appeal to the reason of their friends among the electorate.

Who would argue, in the face of the negative inaction of even those calling themselves militants, that women truly and earnestly accept the theory that militant tactics will win the vote, let alone that which the vote stands for—woman's freedom, of which the vote is the symbol? If the bloody spirit of barbarian ages were, by some hellish means, to be revived among the W.S.P.U. no one would say that the women might not conquer.

We do not believe—there is no evidence to induce us to believe—that that dark spirit may be revived in English women. We do not believe that there is any excuse for any suggestion of reviving it. The men who understand woman's right to the suffrage have not been led so to understand by violence; those who remain hostile will never be taught the reason of woman's right except by reasoning; and what humanity needs beyond all things is an understanding between men and women, a mutual tolerance of each other's particular desires.

Militant tactics have proved a failure. They were a resort to an obsolete roughness which has been trained smooth for centuries now in the class of women from whence the W.S.P.U. members are mostly drawn. The leaders themselves have done nothing more militant than minor assault. They have not been "tempted" even by the spectacle of their "outraged and inhumanly tortured" followers. It is time they ceased egging the others on!

WOMEN AND FREEDOM

D. Triformis

The New Age, May 12, 1910

BY AN ADMIRABLE article Miss Jane Harrison assuages my despair of the "Englishwoman." Let us pray that this may set a standard which will forbid that journal to harbour such heroines as Mrs. Rentoul Esler's Celestine, whose young man won her with the following words: "Princess, in my dreams I only aspire to carpet the ground you tread. My hopes do not lift themselves to the level of your heart."[1]

Miss Harrison saves the situation this month. She writes on "Heresy and Humanity."[2] "The gist of heresy," she says, "is free personal choice in act and in thought, the rejection of traditional faiths and customs, qua traditional." Note that "personal choice in thought." It is a distinguished phrase. "Herd suggestion is always in a haze." "We are humane so far as we are conscious or sensitive to the individual life. Patriotism is collective herd instinct, it is repression of individuality. You feel strongly because you feel alike, you are reinforced by the other homogeneous units, you sing the same song, you wave

---

[1] Erminda Rentoul Esler, an Irish romance novelist.

[2] Jane Ellen Harrison, a classical scholar whose lecture "Heresy and Humanity" was given in Cambridge on December 7, 1909, and subsequently reprinted in the periodical *The Englishwoman.*

the same flag. Humanity is sympathy with infinite differences, with utter individualism, with complete differentiation, and it is only possible through the mystery of organic spiritual union. We have come most of us now to a sort of physical union by sympathy and imagination. To torture even an enemy's body would be to us physical pain, physical sickness; there will come the day when to hurt mentally and spiritually will be equally impossible, because the mental and spiritual life will be one."

I hope this is not too much liberty taken in quoting. My intentions are good. I must not go very far as if in comment, however, as Miss Harrison's elaboration of her all too brief article might be very different from mine. It is my desire to dwell upon the phrase "personal choice in thought," for that seems to me to describe the starting point of freedom; and we may find the principle of freedom here. Physical freedom may well march around and wave a flag, dancing for very joy of unchained limbs. Released convicts and slaves fittingly breathe deep and set off somewhere at a run. But mental freedom is a different thing and has different attributes, inward and invisible, corresponding to the outward and visible manner of its advent. Physical freedom may be given from without. Mental freedom must be begotten from within. Thought begets it; and its only outward evidence is personal choice—a happy, but never a noisy, thing. The woman who is mentally free, knowing how imperceptible is the evolution of this freedom, knows, also, that to try and impart the free mind to a person who wants still to be shouting and waving a flag would be of as much use as to fasten a wing upon a lizard and bid it be a bird and fly.

Women who imagine that by herding themselves in large numbers and parading the streets, they are proving their right to freedom, are actually proving that they are a herd with that subconscious distrust of reason which has always distinguished herds and mobs. Mobs do not believe in the way of reason; they believe in noise and banners and the power of money. We are soon to have a procession of the W.S.P.U. costing, says Mrs. Pethick

Lawrence,[3] a thousand pounds. We are to have "banners and colours in our Procession surpassing all that has ever been seen before." Now, will you say we have no right to the vote? A thousand pounds—twenty-seven bands—banners that beat everything!

The W.S.P.U. are fond of quoting Christ, that Example of violence, to excuse their tactics. One cannot at least imagine Christ going round for money to help His cause, or to buy banners surpassing all that has ever been seen before. The revelations concerning the Salvation Army are a current proof of the impossibility of keeping the spiritual force clear when commercialism—salvation shops, salvation tea, salvation uniforms, etc.—has once got a footing in a movement. And commercialism has been introduced into the women's movement by the Women's Social and Political Union. As Mrs. Pethick Lawrence so enthusiastically voices it, "Self-denial week is a week of sacrifice that will be expressed in the precise and definite terms of silver and gold." Aye! and what we shall get for it will be a Procession, etc., etc., etc. But we shall not buy freedom, for freedom is not to be expressed in terms of silver and gold.

It may be asserted that some practical reforms have needed money to bring them about. If the case is challenged and examples are given, I shall be delighted to analyse the subject. Yet I imagine that few persons will need more than their own sense of right to show them the difference between the commercial appeal of, for instance, Dr. Barnardo,[4] and all he could do with money and the commercial appeal of Mrs. Pethick Lawrence and all she can do with money.

And what is to be our next move towards Freedom—the capital letter here!—if we cannot appeal with our twenty-seven bands to "the conscience of those who would keep us in subjection while they exploit and degrade our sex"? Our answer

---

[3] Emmeline Pethick Lawrence, co-editor of *Votes for Women*.
[4] Thomas John Barnardo, Irish philanthropist who founded homes for poor children.

comes from the same noble pen. "Wage unceasing warfare until women enter upon their inheritance, and the victory is won." That means we shall begin slapping and pushing again; and that, further interpreted, means that unless we provide gladiatorial shows for our supporters, the W.S.P.U. will soon be forgotten. Our friends the Police will keep order for the sake of the city while we turn it into a fair. They are well trained, these police. They will even keep order for the sake of the city while we are turning it into a Donnybrook. And in thus keeping order between us and an electorate that does not wish to have us shouting at it in the streets, they are obeying a Government which is obviously more in line with civilisation than are the rioters. For let us understand that it is not Mr. Churchill or Mr. Anybody in the Government who mobs the suffrage meetings. It is the electorate—yes, this same electorate that fought for its own enfranchisement because being composed of men it could fight, and besides, was not averse from violence. We, as women, are averse from violence. The women who do not feel disgust at physical combat are but a handful compared to the number of women in this country who dislike the methods of violence, and many of whom the acts of the militant suffragettes have driven into actual opposition to their own enfranchisement. The militants do not hesitate to mention the French Revolution and to talk glibly of bloodshed. "We hope politicians will not force women to bloodshed." Who is going to shed this blood? Mrs. Pethick Lawrence? It is not likely; but some half-daft listener, drinking in the suggestion, may commit the crime which will land her in a criminal lunatic asylum. One cannot readily believe that our great Leader or our dear Treasurer has ever really read a history of the French Revolution; for, otherwise, their utterances about it must be termed as one would not care to term them.

But let us get away from these abominations. Freedom, won in such ways, is not the freedom for which women are seeking.

We are not bodily slaves. No man forces us to marry, nor does the Government send its police to drag us back to a husband we dislike. Bodily free, then, all the slavery we endure we endure because our minds are not free. When we think freely we shall choose freely, we shall act freely; but "personal choice in thought" is the first condition of acting freely. No man can give us that mental freedom, but with mental freedom gained from within ourselves, we should scarcely fail to convince our fathers and brothers of our right to the vote. Everything we might say or do would assist us, if we were mentally free. Men are contemptuous now of our conventions, our superstitions, our prohibitive and censorious preferences. That can scarcely be too often repeated, for this contempt is at the bottom of men's opposition. Our own minds must free us since our own minds enslave us. When Miss Beatrice Tina wrote: "The militant suffragettes have saved us from the last ignominy of the slave—the obligation to give thanks for enfranchisement,"[5] she penned, though in a spirited style, one of the most foolish fancies of the average thoughtless woman. It seems positively dear to some women to think of themselves as the revolting slaves of men. That parrot phrase, proper enough for a slave, is improper for a woman, and doubtless it has done its mischief among women. But if we set our minds upon becoming free from within, we shall see that such epigrams, though fascinating, are untrue.

One of the difficult things in the world is to review one's life, dispassionately reflecting and dispassionately approving or condemning. Yet a little time, daily, given to this purpose would soon discover to us those occasions upon which we have acted freely; and it would both invigorate and calm us to find, as we should find, that our lives had been largely self-controlled. In striving to become mentally free, it is of importance to reject, for

---

[5] This is the last sentence of "Woman as a State Creditor" in *Woman's Worst Enemy: Woman.* See page 42.

the time being, outside influence. We must stand, each one, by herself. I quote Miss Harrison again, but, again, I am bound to remind readers that she may utterly disagree with my conclusions. "So long as we will not trouble to know exactly and intimately, we may not, must not choose." We must, that is, for safety, follow the herd. Individuals, people who know themselves are neither content to be herded nor to be the leaders of herds. For the herd seeks only its self-interest. We need not turn further than to this same number of the "Englishwoman" to see how hard herd proclivities die.

In an article on the franchise in New Zealand, Lady Stout[6] has the following paragraph:—"We seem to be able to get any measures we want through our vote. We have, of course, the right to stand for any educational, charitable aid or benevolent board, or municipal office, but women seldom avail themselves of the opportunity. We are all so busy in our domestic life that we cannot find time for public duties that can be performed by men who are elected by our votes." Women in New Zealand have gained absolute control over their own money, a definite share of a deceased husband's money, equal divorce rights, and have raised the standard of women's wages. But to men, whom they could not trust to do any of these great public services, the women, with faith truly touching, leave the educational, charitable, benevolent, and municipal drudgery.

Dear, dear! And to remember that our own W.S.P.U. has just these same ends in mind and is not identified with a single humanitarian project. There is probably not one humanitarian or charitable movement which has not suffered through the money given towards votes for women. But what would you? We must have our thousand-pound-Procession. That way lies Freedom!

---

[6] Anna Paterson Stout, suffrage activist from New Zealand.

WOMEN AND FREEDOM

Beatrice Hastings

The New Age, May 19, 1910[1]

TO The Editor of "The New Age."

I certainly do not wish to be named with those who creep away from a public criticism; but the fact is I have no defence to make for my unlucky epigram. I admit that it is not true as it stands, and that the idea (unexpressed) in my mind at the time was certainly of "mental" freedom, and then I am bound to agree with D. Triformis that mental freedom must be gained by thought. I have learned a good deal from D. Triformis and I hope I may learn more; but some things I have not to learn. I have long since protested against several of the undesirable aspects of the suffrage movement. In a reply to Mr. G. K. Chesterton I wrote: "The real question of women's suffrage is whether it will lead to progressive or to reactionary legislation." Later I objected to the way certain notoriously narrow-minded suffragists used the name of Mary Wollstonecraft and distorted her ideals; and further, I complained of the growing mercenary spirit among so-called advanced women. I have not complained publicly, hitherto, about

---

[1] Hastings wrote this letter, as Beatrice Hastings, in response to the essay "Women and Freedom," which she had written one week earlier as D. Triformis.

the official boycott of my book,[2] partly because it sold all the same; but I am a living example for D. Triformis of the "prohibitive and censorial preferences" she notices among the leaders of the various sections. For all these reasons she need not have thrust me out as merely a foolish woman. One is not altogether foolish who has been killed for speaking the truth. It is also a distinction to be the only woman in England who does not want a family. No, I am not altogether silly. I should feel more of a laughing stock for the immortals if I had given sons to a State which might hang my son for some sudden act due to his inheriting my own and my father's temper. I resent the lies about marriage which I was allowed to grow up believing, and my ignorant and unwilling maternity I regard as an outrage. For saying these things I was cast out by advanced women. "Votes for Women" would not even mention that it had received a copy of my book. At a Fabian soirée I was cut by at least a dozen women, and I resigned my membership, not wishing to contaminate these noble creatures who of course have, all of them, forty children each.

Well, it is the fate of martyrs to be subsequently canonised. Meanwhile, D. Triformis may well spare me from her gallery. I have been killed out of the "advanced" movement. I now devote myself in the shades to art and humanitarianism. *De mortuis nil nisi bonum.*[3]

BEATRICE (TINA) HASTINGS

---

[2] *Woman's Worst Enemy: Woman.*
[3] Say nothing but good of the dead.

PARODIES OF EZRA POUND & FUTURISM

THE WAY BACK TO AMERICA

T.K.L.

From September 4 through October 16, 1913, The New Age published a series of seven essays by Ezra Pound about contemporary French poetry entitled "The Approach to Paris." Beginning with this essay on September 18, Hastings wrote a series of parodies of Pound's essays under the pseudonym "T.K.L.," which she had previously used for other satirical pieces. Hastings ended up writing six parodies of Pound from September 18 through October 30, and two of those pieces are reproduced here. For a more thorough account of the Pound-Hastings showdown in The New Age, *see Sunny Stalter-Pace's essay in this book.*

The New Age, September 18, 1913

ATTENDEZ, mes enfants! I am about to waste ten minutes in exposition of the so-called English poets. What I have to say is brief, pardieu! They were all French! Who is that interrupting? Ha—you wish to infer that Chaucer wrote no poetry until he forgot he had once been in France? Well, you may infer what you please, I suppose. What? The "Canterbury Tales"? I smile explosively—all pure French, my dear sir! Now sit down and let me talk. Shakespeare owed all his technique to the Pléiade, that miraculous constellation of Frenchmen. Shakespeare invoked sleep:

Canst thou upon the high and giddy mast[1]
Seal up the ship-boy's eyes and rock his brains
In cradle of the rude, imperious surge?

You hear his origins, n'est ce pas? Enough. Ex pede Herculem! They
have had a poet, one Swinburne. He, choice creature, enlightened
these English. Before Swinburne they believed that a poet should
say something! The French of A.D. 1300 had failed to show them
the beauty of mere emotional words, divine, unphilosophical. Ha—
but exoticism, exoticism! Pardon! I am grieving for Alexandria, for
Babylon, for Catulle, Catulle! You, perhaps, don't catch on, but do
as you please! To-day, once again, we make a trade of art. We know
our tools. We can sit down to our business as deliberately as any
other craftsman and make good. Muses? Ah, the brave jest! Muses!
My friends, we are the Muses. I myself will muse for you to order,
and do it superlatively. My personal circle is small—I am an exile
on this planet—yet no country, except perhaps England—I know
nothing for certain—is altogether alien to me; I find always one
choice creature in the trade. We meet. He and I then construct
la poèsie, ours or another's or each other's. Two tinkers can each
construct an admirable tin can. Two poets can each sing admirably
about a tin can, I suppose. We do not sing of tin cans, but we could
if we liked. That we sing Beauty, pur et simple, is because it is
better for trade. You do not take me? Consider it—not too literally
please—at your leisure. I have a brother in art. I admire him. He
handles his tools. Perhaps I exaggerate, but I honestly believe he
has recovered the aesthetic grand mystery—no mystery at all really,
but as good as, being so long forgotten. My brother is French,
but you guessed this! His wave-lengths! Long! Don't mention it.
They need never stop. They only do stop, because it is better for
trade. Think over this! He knows more about verse-rhythm than
any man living—and why should he not, since nobody else knows

---

[1] These lines are from *Henry IV, Part 2*, although Hastings has changed
the word "Wilt" to "Canst."

more than he knows? No one else knows anything whatever about his rhythms, for they are his own, incomparable. Them that do assume, ignorant, shallow, have dragged up comparisons. They may compare, of course. I am not God.

> Cow hypocrite,[2]
> Cow of pretence.
> Cow colour of fawn, more fraudulent than our nags, cow
>   colour of fawn, bedaubed with brush, walking lie,
>   cow hypocrite, cow of pretence.
> Cow erst in a pound, footsore down at St. Louis, cow
>   erst in a pound, now corned and in tins at Paris,
>   cow hypocrite, cow of pretence.
> Cow of visage rouged, Boodle a business man, cow of
>   visage rouged, was spoofed by the paint on your
>   skin, cow hypocrite, cow of pretence.
> Cow with black eyes, the fatuous mug made a deal, cow
>   with black eyes, gave you the run of his patch, cow
>   hypocrite, cow of pretence.
> Cow colour of gold, next day he urged his friends to
>   inspect his purchase, cow colour of gold, they spat,
>   these Americans ten, cow hypocrite, cow of pretence.
> Cow like spotted pard, you should have hitched out of
>   shot, cow like spotted pard, each spit become a
>   splotch, cow hypocrite, cow of pretence.

———◆———

Take breath, mes enfants, though there is more to come. If you are not too drunk with the delicate stuff to be able to carry it as if, as if, I repeat, unconcerned, you will wake at the end of the reading to

---

[2] Hastings parodies Remy de Gourmont's poem "Litanies de la Rose" (opening lines: "Fleur hypocrite, / Fleur du silence."), which Pound quotes at great and untranslated length in his "Approach to Paris" essay from September 11, 1913.

know that the pageant of all the subtle, neglected, misunderstood poets that ever were has passed before you. You agree? You agree because you also are in the trade. If it were otherwise, I could not have shown you all the elegances of my brother's technique. If there be a man here incapable of yearning over this I cannot help it. If he says that all these assonances are merely decadent exaggerations of one part of the whole technique of poetry, if he considers that rhyme, such as Shakespeare caught has its place—

> Come away, come away, Death,[3]
> And in sad cypress let me be laid;
> Fly away, fly away, breath;
> I am slain by a fair cruel maid.
> My shroud of white stuck all with yew,
> O! prepare it.
> My part of death, no one so true
> Did share it.
>
> Not a flower, not a flower sweet,
> On my black coffin let there be strown;
> Not a friend, not a friend greet
> My poor corse, where my bones shall be thrown.
> A thousand thousand sighs to save,
> Lay me, O! where
> Sad true lover never find my grave,
> To weep there.

—if he says that in this lyric both assonance and rhyme are beautifully mingled, and that my brother's poem is like a boy's trick, again I cannot help it.

> Cow grey as a shirt, you weren't worth a greenback
> washed, cow grey as a shirt, Boodle cursed in his
> wrath, cow hypocrite, cow of pretence.

---

[3] This song is from *Twelfth Night*.

> Cow of innocent soul, at auction you fetched forty-five,
>> cow of innocent soul, (cents) it was not your fault,
>> cow hypocrite, cow of pretence.
> Cow doomed, the butcher, the packer, the grocer, cow
>> doomed, slew, put and sold you in can, cow
>> hypocrite, cow of pretence.

Ah—it begins to tell on you, but I love your drooping! I must explain that whereas this traduction of mine appears to show connected idea, the French original transcends all such commonplace, but what would you? I am employing English and the tongue makes for mere sense. It has hitherto defeated almost all its poets, these, no doubt, true enough yearners after Beauty, pur et simple. Just look at their piteous stolid fabrics woven, malgré eux, around their blockish skylarks, Satans, Pilgrims, scholar gypsies and what not. My brother's ineffable words mean anything you like, cows, roses, toads, dairymaids or queens—if you must have a meaning, but why have one?

In French the thing is a marvel. Listen!

> Fleur hypocrite,
> Fleur du silence.
> Rose couleur de cuivre, plus frauduleuse que nos
> joies, rose couleur de cuivre, embaume-nous dans tes
> mensonges, fleur hypocrite, fleur du silence.

But imagine an Englishman to set down the stuff! The pure article!

> Hypocritical flower,
> Flower of the silence.
> Copper-coloured rose, more fraudulent than our joys,
> copper-coloured rose, embalm us in thy lies, hypocritical
> flower, flower of the silence.

But you can't imagine it! Such sublime language were only to be ventured upon by a few exquisite souls—and they are all in

Bedlam! Such is England! Condole with me, and do forget the impossible Saxon and take to French.

> Cow transfigured, prime peach-fed pig you in tin, cow
> transfigured, sold in Paris for three times your
> carcase's price, cow hypocrite, cow of pretence.
> Cow, cow, those Gauls, those applauding messieurs,
> loved you, hugged you, swallowed you, abolished
> all cruder foods, cow, cow, resolved to bless
> America with their presence and never to forget
> Yankee- doodle, cow hypocrite, cow of pretence.
> Cow, cow, cow, cow, cow, your return to the land of your
> birth, with glory galore is certain if you spurn the
> sordid hang-dog mob of English critics and
> whipster versifiers, cow, cow, cow, cow, cow, I can
> drag this out as long as I wish and term my
> amateur spurts perfectly :brand-new verse-
> rhythms and be apotheosised by novelty-mongers,
> but I prefer my supper which stands served in a
> hot dish, cow hypocrite, cow of pretence.

My brother's latest achievement is the "Sonnets in Prose," to be followed by "Lyrics in Prose," and the series will culminate in "Poetry in Prose," only to introduce a second series—"Novels in Poesie," "Encyclopaedias in Poesie," "Essays in Poesie," and so on. You see, friends, if we can only mix everything up and break every law of the common aesthetic, it will be much better for the trade. It irks me and my brothers to have to compete on their own lines with those servile poets who studied fitness and actually threw away in their ridiculous pride hundreds of experiments which in their estimation would never lead to poetical success, but which we have picked up and shall offer to the public, willy nilly. But, friends, it'll be willy, n'est ce pas?

ALL EXCEPT ANYTHING

T.K.L.

The New Age, October 16, 1913

READER, when I began these articles I had no notion that there were so many Frenchmen! I thought they were doing these things better in France. But, alas, France is swarming: and every second individual is a poet exactly as over here in these chilly, but prolific, islands. Exactly, too, as over here every one of these poets is unique, incomparable, defiant of computation; every one makes his poems his very own; every one challenges in his especial person all the old poets and poetical trappings; every one sings of the commonplace, the ordinary you and the ordinary me, and particularly of the ordinary young female person; every one talks "normally" instead of posing as a Bard; every one prints his Bare Statement of Things in metrical lines. It begins to beat me to know one from another in spite of the fact that they are all unique. Wherein, then, shall I seek and find, as I must, the distinction of the so distinguished Monsieur Jammes? Let me begin by saying what he is not, and what he does not do.

M. Jammes[1] is not a Pindarist. He does not celebrate the Grand Prix by a yell for some god to dignify the "lofty

---

[1] Francis Jammes, French poet and subject of a previous Unsung Masters book.

strain." His strains are not "lofty." You may excuse Pindar's invocation, perhaps on the grounds which you would allow to an archbishop who should include Jehovah in a religious celebration. Pindar believed in the deities of the Hellenes, actually believed that their aid was essential both in war and in those martial exercises, the Olympic Games. The victor always and everywhere owed his success to a well-spent life under godly direction. Hence the deific invocations! To-day, very few people believe that God is present at the Grand Prix. To be sure you may often hear that congregation invoking every god ever heard of, and as many devils; but something, je ne sais quoi, informs our souls that those Grand Prix deities have another odour than Pindar's gods had for him, or even for the uninitiated Olympic multitudes. Even on secular grounds, Jammes is all there not to imitate the old bards. In days when the bard, Homer, for instance, actually toyed with the plectrum, or flattered the Pythian victor (like Pindar), or presented a tragedy with masks (like Sophocles), someone was probably tickled to death, or their sporting instincts were flattered, or they were paid to attend, like the Paris claque. Anyway, it was the fashion of the time for bards to ramp about. It is not the fashion now, and so Jammes doesn't ramp about. You may say, if you wish to say something, that our own times are full of large event, procession, and catastrophe. I reply that the Poets of our times do not think so. They have a new perspective. The common, the so-called "trivial," is now seen by them to be the one thing that is really poetical. In England as well as in France, in America as well as in Germany and Bengal, we sing now the eternal Trifle. It is not my doing, is it? I merely state the fact that poetical perspective has changed! Not for Jammes, that almighty pose of Pindar—the tongue of Jove! Not for Jammes the Muse, the lofty poet's Lyre of Language, the Singing Robes of inspiration. Jammes knows nothing of these appurtenances, and is not going to pretend that he does.

I may as well leave negativising Jammes and tell you what he does contain. I have shown you Remy de Gourmont, Imagiste; Vildrac, Humaniste; Tailharde, Plelleniste; Romains, Unanimiste, and others, each one in his own unique way bent upon clarifying poetic diction, making a plain statement and scheduling his times for posterity. But to Jammes I allot a special niche upon the new Parnassus, for Jammes is more uniquely unique than—I had nearly said—than any other living French poet, but we must conserve our plaudits—any of the above-mentioned unique poets; he makes things more his own than I can express; he has perfected the new perfection of being a man in the street; he is your very ordinary self, your office-boy, your office, your telephone, your insurance card, and your stamp! He is the great eliminator of the abstract, the general, the universal, the essential, the transcendental—but he is the grand recorder of the Detail! Jammes has written a novel in verse, detailing life in every small town in France. Think of that!

To write a novel in verse as a series of scenes is nothing new or strange. True, it has hardly been done successfully since Puedeser, and even of him a few people said that he tied up his cow's tail with blue ribands and so set folk laughing at the naturally respectable creature. So it is said to-day that Mr. Jammes has made the provinces of France appear absurdly aspiring and precious, the which they are not, but just common, by printing the daily round of their dull histories in metric lines. People will always be saying something. Jammes, nevertheless, writes his novel in verse. He sees, like all modern poets, an immature female person—

> This child will be stupid
> As these other folk, like her father and mother,
> And yet she has an infinite grace.
> In her is the intelligence of beauty.
> How delicious! her breast that does not exist,

Her back and her feet. But she will be stupid
As a goose in two years from now.[2]

"Elle sera bête comme une oie dans deux ans d'ici." You see I have
not absurdly exalted the poet in translating him. One is tempted.
There above is no word you or I might not have said to one
another. Jammes always uses our language! Consider that miracle
of simple and adequate statement in the scene where Madame
Larribeau discovers her husband's infidelity with the servant. The
poor woman sobs "Gueu, gueu, gueu..." thirty-five times.[3] Jammes
writes them all down. It is all exactly like a realistic novel and done
to the life. Jammes is a Detailist, and every single one of Madame's
noises is to him a natural and mentionable Detail. Now I think of
Naturalism. Shall I therefore call Monsieur Jammes a Naturaliste?
Why not? He is a Naturaliste. He mentions everything. He is a
Mentionaliste. He is a part of our normal life. He is a Normaliste.
He produces in his poems the effect of a conversation. He is a
Conversationaliste. He says something—so few people do! He is
a Somethingaliste. And now, perhaps, we have Jammes. I think I
have said that M. Jammes can touch nothing without making it his
own. Yes, I have certainly said that. I will say some more about it.
It is, I think, the great gift. It is "style" in the fine sense. It is, in the
fine sense, literature. Now, perhaps, we have our Gift. M. Jammes
makes the famous pilgrimage to Lourdes his own, every detail of it.
He looks, sees, and writes down a simple statement. He has the art
of the Prosie; he writes prose in metrical lines! Many other poets
of to-day do this. Jammes does it as only Jammes can! You must be
subtle to discern the difference between Jammes' prosies and the
prosies of, say, my friend Vildrac. If you are subtle you will note

---

[2] Hastings refers to Jammes's poem "La jeune fille," which Pound
quotes and discusses at length in his installment of "The Approach to
Paris" on October 9, 1913.
[3] Here Hastings parodies a passage from Jammes's verse-novel
Existences, which Pound also discusses in his essay.

Jammes' especial and unique use of rhyme. A man deaf to all rhyme save cat-and-bat will obviously fail to hear Jammes' rhymes, he will fancy Jammes is not rhyming at all, or he will fancy that Jammes is murdering assonance. I invite to listen them that comprehend the beauty of such tonal delicacies or the delicacies of such tonal beauties, whichever you will, as drapeaux—en or; soit-il mourir; serait-ce que—priait Dieu—these a few of Jammes' line-endings.

Except for the rhyme, the poem on the pilgrimage would have passed for a mere ordinary prosie—

> Les drapeaux,
> se penchaient avec leur devises en or.
> Le soleil était blanc sur les escaliers,
> dans l'air bleu, sur les clochers déchiquetés.

> The banners
> hung down with their devices of gold.
> The sun was white on the stairways,
> in the blue air, on the jagged belfries.

These delicate rhymes are as close as I can reproduce those of M. Jammes. But what a plain statement! It is as clear as a "news-story"; it is the plainest prose. But Jammes prints it in metric. Do not ask me why. I do not explain Jammes. He prints it in metric! With small letters at the beginnings of lines. Eccentric? I repeat that I do not explain. Jammes, reporting, is not a mere reporter. I suggest that the average reporter does not arrange his "news-story" in metric lines, whereas Jammes does. Jammes does and becomes a poet. Your reporter does not, and remains a reporter. The metric line is a recognised property of poets. If the above were set straight along, how would one know that it was a poem? The rhymes alone would not sufficiently mark it; they are too delicate. But I object to appearing to defend Jammes. I put the proposition that one of the laws of poetry may be that prose shall be printed in metrical lines (and called Prosie), and pass on. "I've seen," writes Jammes—

> I've seen in old galleries Flemish pictures
> where, in a dark inn, one saw a type...
> qui buvait de la biére, et sa très mince pipe
> avait un point rouge, et il fumait doucement...
> that sat drinking beer, and his slender pipe
> had markings of red, and he smoked at his ease.
> She gave them some broth, without any bread,
> And whipped them all soundly...

In English this metre is old and sacred to doggerel. But Jammes writes in French! He gives you the Detail, the unadulterated, unsentimental, simple, adequate Detail. Some think of Jammes as the dullest dog that ever wrote anywhere but in England, as of an incessant and pretentious talker, talking in verse, talking of the obvious, talking, talking, talking, dropping his rhymes like a dude dropping his aitches, insisting on his small letters like a provincial insisting on his burr, staring at everything with the greed of a youth making his living with a Kodak, as of a rude, intrusive, eavesdropping, scandalous, relentless bore. Personally, I find that he gives me distinct pleasure. I have seen lots of the details he mentions. I have, for instance, seen just such an inn as he describes. He freshens my memory. I have, also, seen and heard just such a young miss as he celebrates—

> "Oh, my dear! Oh! la la...
> ...Just imagine...on Tuesday
> I saw him...I l-laughed! She talks
> Like that.

Jammes has written "The Life of a Passionate Young Girl," also "The Life of an Ancient Young Girl." In each case he gives us the Detail and abjures the Whole. You might think you were reading Mr. W. W. Gibson; just as in reading M. Tailharde, you think he is Mr. Aleister Crowley; M. Vildrac—Mr. Yeats; M. Romains—Mr. James Stephens; M. de Gourmont—Mr. Arthur Symons. In so supposing you would be neglecting the nuances! I have not, however, said that Jammes is the very greatest living poet. I don't know that I shall do so even now. I don't think I shall ever say another word about him.

WAKE UP, ENGLAND!

T.K.L.

The New Age, June 25, 1914

CUTTING THE CACKLE, I remark that we Futurists[1] have introduced into modern painting four new elements which are changing rapidly all over Europe the preconceived notion of what a picture should be! This preconceived notion is the preconceived notion you have taken from the artists of the past. We have an entirely new notion for immediate circulation. It is not exactly the business of the painter to explain himself in words; but you seem unable to understand our notion from our paintings, and we must sell!

Firstly, then, no picture should be a mere representation! This is new. We have just discovered it. The photograph, the cinema, have outdone mere representation! A photograph of Rembrandt would outdo Rembrandt's portrait of himself. That little machine would get more out of Rembrandt in two ticks than all Rembrandt's genius could select in a life-time. What number of Romneys would we not exchange for a photo of Lady Hamilton? How the camera would have induced from her all which Romney missed, and the lack of which leaves Emma Hamilton so much antique lumber on our hands!

---

[1] In this piece, Hastings parodies Futurist manifestos.

Take, now, the topographical record. It reproduces a scene much quicker and much better than any artist might, just as the camera reproduces a face. We Futurists say that a picture must be the plastic abstraction of an emotion! What emotion is there in any scene ever painted? But think of the cinema representations of scenery. The very trees rush across the landscape! Trains, motor-cars move, and it is only necessary to have a man at the back, rattling gravel, for us to get the absolute emotion of speed. Even Turner's train gives nobody this emotion! Some critics say that Turner's train gives just this emotion, that one feels there the tenseness of a thing moving at its highest possible speed, that one is not outside and a mere spectator as at the cinema where the vehicles rush past one, but inside and only less identified with the motion than men are identified with the motion of the planet. These people are, of course, wrong!

In painting by means of abstractions, forms, colours, dimensions, that do not imitate natural forms, it is possible to create emotions infinitely more stimulating than those created by contemplating nature! Abstractions, of course, are not in nature. We Futurists are not in nature. We are outside nature, which is only moons and moans and old ruins, and not planes and dimensions and speed and that sort of thing. Turner's speed is, of course, a delusion. You have only to look at one of our Futurist pictures of speed to see and feel the real thing—everybody and things whirling—zang! boom! zing!—you can almost hear the man with the gravel!!

Our second discovery is that art must be the expression, intensification, and concentration of life! Some artists like to consider art as something solemn, exquisite, apart from life! This proves that our discovery is really quite new, and that no artist hitherto has related art to life. We have thus introduced an entirely new element into painting!!

Our third new element is that art must be an intensification of life, therefore of modern life, of which the chief and distinctive feature is speed!

The chief and distinctive feature of modern machinery—no, no, of modern life, Life!—is speed.

Look how we pop across the Atlantic in five days—less! We go for the sake of the speed. For instance, Mr. Oilibank has entirely altered his character from what it was ten years ago. He pops across now to see how fast he can go! He don't want to do anything else, bless you. He lives for speed. Speed is his life. Speed has displaced in him all his old outworn human plottings and plannings. Oilibank is no more a Prop of the Empire and a man; he has become a geometric splendour, a pure, the purest of machines, and the chief and distinctive feature of his life—Life!— is speed. In intensifying mechanical speed in our paintings, we give you, therefore, a true idea of modern life.

This leads to our fourth new element—the painting of the "states of mind"; that is to say, we claim that by means of contrasted colours, lines, and dimensions, it is possible to give the artist's various states of mind! This is supremely important, as every woman would admit. Some people would, of course, object that the artist is not concerned with his states of mind, but with statements of his mind. And these will be the persons who accuse us of being petty and ill-balanced.

The fact is that our work is, above all, the lyrical and emotional expression of our time, which is a mechanical age, and therein lies its whole beauty! We are not to be deceived by the machine-minder's apparent human squirmings and struggles the while he is being geometrically splendidised. The glory of this age is machinery. We Futurists glorify mechanism. All that's wanted is more of it. The Trade Unions are combining for this end.

Art is not a narcotic, it is not a drug, but a stimulant; not a soporific, but a tonic. This is to imply that other art than the new art has been, of course, narcotic, soporific. And we do imply this. What has art done, hitherto, but kept us down, yearning, searching after Nature and moons! Ha! movement for Us! The motor-'bus, the yellow, green, and crimson taxis gliding like snakes through the limousine! Why, Nature and the old Art have brought things to such a pass that it is actually necessary to bully people into liking a charming city like London, where there is more machinery than the world has ever seen!

I pass on from what will doubtless be a work of time for us Futurists, namely, to turn the spirit of man from wishing to hitch his wagon to a star instead of to a motor-engine. There will always remain a few dreamy people who, amidst chromatic crowds, scarlet taxis, and highly coloured advertisements, are not there! It is the poets we have to watch against. We are, however, now getting a competent staff of Futurist poets who will help to knock out the old nonsense!!

People should constantly buy new pictures. A picture should never be lived with. Who could live with any picture ever painted? Live, eating, drinking, sleeping, sitting, smoking, staring every instant at one picture? I, for instance, wouldn't have the Monna Lisa as a gift! Simply because I have seen her smile reproduced all round Europe. Of course, there is no difference between the smile as painted by Da Vinci and that reproduced by the camera! As an artist, I stake my reputation on this. But the point is that people should be constantly buying pictures; this is better for all parties. And an artist should advertise! Selfridge advertises!![2] No doubt, much old work is as living to-day as it ever was. But it is impossible to get inspiration from it, even although it is as living to-day as it ever was. Perhaps it never was!

This concludes my remarks, except that it is useless for artists to ignore the Press just as it is useless for journalists to ignore the general public—that advanced and intelligent body beginning to realise that what England to-day is to the Past, the Futurists now are to England!

---

[2] Selfridges, a chain of department stores founded in London in 1909.

Beatrice Tina
The New Age, December 10, 1908

METAMORPHOSIS

The foul Apollonian enchanter
Has laid upon me his dark finger:
Know ye not—ceaselessly bleating—
Me, my companions?
See ye not, under these forehead locks,
Fire of the eyes of Chloe?
Hath not my mouth aught familiar,
Bleeding to utter its secret?
Pass ye not by! Shall Selene
Gaze on me, beaten, encysted
Thus in this bovine?
Loose me, ye daughters, now leaping,
Beating these hoofs on your haunches:
Thrust me back, tear from this carcase
Wool, skin, horns—all that disguises!
Shriek out, ye nymphs, your wild laughter,
Seeing this blood blush the thicket,
And the wool of this hide, on the bramble
Float like a flake of the winter.
Tear me, ye tender nurses!
With beautiful hands break asunder—
Room, room for Chloe, Bacchante,
To hurl her white limbs ere the Sun set!

Beatrice Tina
The New Age, May 20, 1909

MIND PICTURES

A brown-skinned boy asleep beneath a clump
Of red-spiked aloe, red the flower;
   A mighty stream, moon-flooded, meeting ocean
   Between two crags which box the encounter
   Of the majestic waters.
What other have I seen in instant flashes?
A woman fleeing, shaking off the shame
Of the hounding dorp,[1] trusting to alien aid,
Fleeing the pointing of the district finger;
   A beggar, catching shell-fish from a rock,
   With nought for all the world to covet,
Nor kith nor kin nor ox nor ass nor anything.

---

[1] A dorp is a village or small town, from the Dutch or Afrikaans.

Beatrice Tina
The New Age, November 25, 1909

VASHTI

Prince beside prince sat when Ahasuerus[1]
    Boasted his queenly gem.
"Summon her!" cried they. "Bring her before us."
    I—to disport for them!

I, Vashti, scorned them. "Return, thou, my answer,
    Briefly, O Memucan,
Say Vashti queries: 'Is left no dancer
    In all of Babylon?'"

Leap! To the walls, ye slaves! Away! blind and halting.
    Kings' horses halt never.
Breathless, the eunuch shall tell my defaulting.
    "O King, live for ever!"

Lonely I wait. Hushed my women around me,
    Hushed all this dais'd room,
Hushed the wild music, as though Death had bound me
    Yesterday! in the tomb.

Courage, heart! Though men may enter this chamber,
    Signing me forth to die—

---

[1] In Chapter One of the Book of Esther, Vashti is the first wife of the Persian king Ahasuerus. She is banished when she refuses to appear at a banquet in order to show off her beauty to the king's guests. Memucan is an advisor of Ahasuerus who suggests Vashti's banishment.

So that, in days to be, none dare remember
    My name was Vashti:

To-night I am Queen! See the blue, green, and white,
    The tassels all golden,
And silk cords of purple. A thousand lamps light
    The Feast I have holden.

Rise up, O Women! and sound out your chorus,
    Lift high each head serene:
Leading the Banquet of Freedom before us,
    Vashti, this night, is Queen.

Beatrice Tina
The New Age, June 9, 1910

BACCHANAL AND NYMPH

He caught one day a Naiad in the cool;
She smoothed her glistening limbs upon a bank.
  He watched her as she formed from out the pool.
  The depth of one brown bulb the water sank.

He asked her whom she loved and who loved her:
She sang a song of wooing Heroes—won!
  A shout from some wild huntsman startled her.
  He loosed her, snatched again, but she was gone.

A bubbling wave be-dimmed the surface gloss.
The bubbles died, yet no nymph did he see.
  He stared where late her form had pressed the moss,
  But there not, nor in all the pool was she.

Beatrice Tina
The New Age, June 9, 1910

NEREID AND BACCHANAL

He called me on from height to height.
The rocks on which we sprung,
Flamed, from his dazzling foot alight—
Fawn of the Ever-Young.

I looked an instant far below.
I saw the awful gulf
Strewn with his lovers, treasure now
For vultures, for the wolf.

"Leap! Leap!" he cried. "Shrink not—but dare!"
"Pity!" I faltered—failed.
Pity! His laughter shocked the air,
And height by height he scaled.

Shine on him, Love! Haste him! Endower!
Joy, pave his Way of Pain!
And leave me Last in the last hour
To fail him once again.

Beatrice Tina
The New Age, June 9, 1910

THE LOST BACCHANTE

We rushed from the forest at break of day,
The last of our mad god's train.
We had wakened the night in cursing the rite
Of a mortal who loves in vain.

I stooped to recover my vest of hide;
They trod me down, triumphing loud:
And there's no reply to my strident cry—
Whither went yon trampling crowd?

My body is red with wounds and rage,
But I'll bathe in the mountain lake,
And I'll ease my spite by blessing the rite
Which the mortal maid did make.

I'll tear me a robe from a tiger's spine,
I'll bind up my ruddy hair
In a band of tendrils plucked from the vine,
And ivy and grapes I will wear.

And I'll leap the meadows towards the city,
Where the mortals dance to-night,
And wrench from the breast of the loved one pity,
And fill it with mad delight.

I'll work in the milky heart of the maid.
With magic I'll ripen her bosom scanty,
Till her lover gasp nor know that he clasp
No mortal maid, but a lost Bacchante.

Beatrice Hastings
The New Age, September 15, 1910

COMRADES

Into the desert I will dare
 My willing foot with you,
If you will give me all my share
 Of toil and danger too.

By the night-fire, beneath the tree
 I'll lightly, lightly sleep,
If you will surely waken me
 The second watch to keep.

Exiled, beside you I will stand,
 Proud in degraded line,
If the same chain which binds your hand
 In tyrant grip, binds mine.

And should fair Fortune send us time
 Of ease and mirthful hours,
And sojourn in some genial clime,
 'Mid singing birds and flowers:

Then up and down the shores we'll rove
 And up and down the vales.
We'll race the winds a-whirl above,
 We'll challenge the swift gales.

In winter-work and summer-play
We'll spend our joy and strength,
Till the soft hand which closes day
Shall lead us home at length.

T.K.L.
The New Age, February 29, 1912

TOM NODDY'S TRUMPET

(Dedicated to John Johnson, trumpeter, ad hoc genus omni.)
   There was a time when witchcraft lent a theme
To Art: when incest and idolatry
Were not disdained by poets: when the free
Delineation of blood-sacrifice, the dream
Of madness, Aphrodite's lash—the stream
Of venomed lust and helpless jealousy—
Seemed subjects fit. Then King Barbarity,
With Ignorance for bugler, reigned supreme.

But now arrives the civilising god
And cracks the trumpet: names the brooding stare
At terrible, excessive things a sign
Of atavism: dockets with the nod
Of science each impassioned, dear nightmare:
And dubs that man diseased whom doodles deem divine.

POST-IMPRESSIONISM

B.H.

The New Age, January 26, 1911

SIR,—The Manniquins wound like a serpent over the grass of the noble domain. They wore something. Madame Valerie in roses, and the two fat German barons, but the Devoted Boy was here and there. Minnie Pinnikin,[1] with flat parted hair, stood on the beautiful vista and cried,

"Desecrators!" Madame Valerie grieved and went down a passage.

————◆————

"But the Beck girls—those puddings!" cried Minnie Pinnikin. "Why should you go to meet them at the docks?—besides, you have never seen them in your life."

"I promised, dear," said Valerie. The Devoted Boy was busy trembling.

————◆————

The Carlton Hotel[2] is much larger than Minnie Pinnikin's flat. "Go and tell that child I'll put her to bed if she doesn't leave off

---

[1] Minnie Pinnikin is also the title character of an unpublished, incomplete novella by Hastings. Excerpts of the text can be found in *Modigliani and the Artists of Montparnasse* by Kenneth Wayne (New York: Harry N. Abrams, 2002).

[2] London luxury hotel. It was later destroyed by bombing in World War II.

shouting down the Carlton stairs," cried Minnie Pinnikin from the lounge to Madame Valerie. "She's to wear whatever there is and a red collar." Minnie Pinnikin then went upstairs herself, and was very agreeable to the sobbing child. It was difficult to choose which crown to wear, all the brims were gone.

———◆———

Minnie Pinnikin's flat's much smaller than the Carlton Hotel. The two fat barons were there and the latter said, "Foh, I don't tell my millionaires!" The Champagne flowed out of the door. Minnie Pinnikin parted her hair very hard and wouldn't join the feast. Valerie was largely everywhere. He wrapped his head in a soft serviette and nursed it on his knee, saying, "Poor old Baron; do take something to eat, Min." So Minnie Pinnikin had a plate on the floor at the knee of the head, and he fed her, horribly goggling "Put these four sprats back," very severely, "it is a sin to waste." "I'm not paying," said the Baron.

———◆———

He was hooking men up from the street. Very surprising the strength of his thin white hands. Everybody was stood upright on the roof of a low house opposite the flat. The loveliest, ready to dance, was like a gipsy angel. Minnie Pinnikin looked out of the window and the flat was empty. "Deserted again," said she; "I'll give twopence." Then they all danced off the roof into the road, and he was obviously and beyond all argument an old-time mummer. "You can't give coppers while the millionaires are looking," said Minnie Pinnikin's husband. Moonbeam child a shadow in the doorway! "Very well, I'll give nothing." Far down in the gutter below the street window the mock curate waved his umbrella. He wound like a serpent. Minnie Pinnikin looked uncompromisingly into his devilish up-goggling orbs. Plumb fell hers into his!

MODERNISM

Alice Morning

The New Age, January 18, 1912

IT WAS VERY LIKE LIFE to find all the swell restaurants in Capetown crowded, the Imperial, the Ritz, Lyons' Pop. and Romano's—all crammed to where the puddings boiled, and none with an electric fan.[1] "Fan I must have," said I; and I dragged him into a side street.

Here there was a fan, and no one in it except ourselves.

Delicious coolness! The chairs extremely antique and highly polished, and the sideboard. The cloth was fresh. All the same, I decided to be careful. "Let me see the visitors' book," I said to the waiter who held a starched and shining serviette.

He brought the book. "Sure you take everyone's name?" I asked. "One does like to know who one's lunching after."

"Yes, madam," he replied, and showed me two names signed in full: "Mr. and Mrs. Cranford." "Very nice people," said the waiter; "often lunch here." "Oh," I exclaimed, "is Mrs. Gaskell with them?" "No, ma'am." "Oh, then, it's not the same Cranfords."

He was stout, of course, but not otherwise. "The Blake Institute?" I cried, as we returned to Piccadilly, keeping on the

---

[1] As Tyler Babbie points out in his essay, the restaurants Hastings lists were located on the Strand in London.

side away from the sea; "that must be a new building." "Not very," he replied; "Queen Anne, about." He grew suddenly emotional. "You-outh, O Mystical Rose!" he exclaimed, stretching his arms: "I knew that building-a when Jenny Lind[2] sang there-a!" "How In-teresting!" I said; "but compose yourself. All is not lost." The Jew shed slow, reproachful tears: "When I saw Jenny Lind descending that sta-hair-case-a, she shimmered like a ro-oose!"

"But even in youth," I said, "even in youth one has to select experience. One cannot have everything. Some things, per-force, must be left undone. So why not make a virtue of it when one is old?"

"Parlez-vous français," said he. "I must—my ancestors were French."

"I can a little," I replied. "Assez pour la rue"—I translated, "enough to go out in the road with, ou magazin, or into a shop, mais pas en philosophe, not like a philosopher."

"Ah, good! I see we shall get on very well."

"So you're going to the Riviera," I exclaimed. "I see the flat's all upside down."

"It's been a trial rummaging all round the Dress Agencies, but I've got a fair haul, enough to last me over my appendicitis."

I didn't care much for the white brocade with cornflowers.

"Those deep black cloth scollops round the hem are too heavy," I suggested; "but try it on."

"Oh, I never try things on," said Valerie, holding the dress against her to show the train. "What's the good—they never fit."

It took us a fortnight to get ready. Mrs. Bates scrubbed the whole flat out every day. "She used to live in the country," Valerie told me. "'Oh, Miss,'" she says, "'the 'oneysuckle!'"

"Why cross the Channel," I suggested, "when we have the Riviera in Cornwall?" So we went to Brighton.

---

[2] Jenny Lind, a 19th century Swedish opera singer.

I was surprised, but I had been to school with her, and the new poet asked me to and seemed dazzled by the sight of a girl seriously interested, but I couldn't make out why the river stopped off sharp. I thought they always slowed off into bogs. But there was the mud. The referee stood between two rocks like Scylla or Charybdis, I forget which, and they had to land there. The first man in sent his boat right on shore and was awfully pleased, but the second boat had two men in, so there was a double disappointment. I had simply to run before the provision shops closed, and I sat on the high stool by the counter and he read it aloud, though the naphtha glittered green.

I knew he was rather taken with me and he came right to the door and upstairs. Polly was quite huffy in a genteel way, but the house was comfortable, even very, and I said, "I always supposed the drawing-room couldn't be on the ground floor." We knew she was an heiress at school, but not how much.

"Come and hear the poems," I said to her; "this Greek God is just down from Oxford and is mad on poetry, always writes every morning, wet or fine."

When it was too late for him to go home we went out to see the wreck. Everybody else was out except Polly. Her dress was very dark and plain, high to the ears.

"I had to take a hat-shop to keep my little boy," she explained; "it was something for him to do minding it when I was out. We had a non-fume-gas-stove, but I spent hundreds of pounds and got bored with it."

"If you had it now," I said, "I could heat this tin of herrings."

Suddenly she rushed to me: "Pops is coming over the water. Oh, do you think he'll get safe to land?" I looked out and saw the abbot rowing like mad, his gown flying all over the boat. He looked quite safe and jolly. Patty blushed. "I call him Pops," she said—"I rather—love him." So I understood at last.

AN AFFAIR OF POLITICS

Alice Morning

The New Age, November 21, 1912

WELL, I said, I could have two boys instead of one of each of the maids and put them to sleep in the harness room the ventilation is perfect but solve the problem I shall it's shameful! I couldn't have them in the house and with a thick carpet on the floor and there is a fireplace everything would be alright. Moore tells me he has seen a hundred and forty-nine guests stopping here and all the maids and valets slept all over those beautiful stables. Doesn't it seem awful! Guy said well let me know dear when you've quite decided but boys and old women are not everybody's fancy which was good news to me I thought the Act would have snapped them all up already before I knew they weren't under it though in that case I should have tried for girls and old men, pay—never that's all. I hated having to ask the guests to walk up to the Castle and Mrs. Follitt swore very because her train got caught in a rabbit trap but all the others said she shouldn't swear the Cause was too admirable and we mustn't be beaten by Liberal chauffeurs! So we get there only a very little dewy and a bit footy with one swamp. And the poor old thing had his gout again and I simply let the nurse make a perfect fool of me because she was wheeling him round one way to receive me and I went the other and I kept on getting at the back of him because of the perfectly awful noise where Henry was having a shooting party in the dining-room, a perfectly ridiculous joke and not at all amusing. And the best of it was while I could see he was as fond of me as ever and never meant to cut me off with nothing but the paddock I simply didn't know what to do about the Guests who Thomas said had all gone by mistake into the servants' new dining-room and were Astonished! I should think so though I love onions and cold beef and great slabs of cheese but he shouldn't be so charitable and have the servants' supper at the usual time with me in an awful state about how he would receive me because he does change his mood ten times a day when his toe is bad poor darling. But fortunately everybody knows the family's mad and when nobody would move I said oh well this is quite charming and let us let the servants go in the dining room and we'll all stop here and eat cheese and we did all except Mrs. Follitt who thought it wasn't right and being a sort of aunt absolutely she went all by herself and stopped Henry's nonsense which was silly of her because Henry always gets quite drunk if he can't do what he likes and positively she sat on the right hand of Thomas and pretended it was Father! Greedy old thing I'm sure if our spread had been in the servants' hall she would have come! Pa really did enjoy it and promised he wouldn't say anything horrid about me and the Act and the paddock although I told him truthfully that Principles at Stake would never let me pay. And there was another upset when we all got back to the Spinney House Emily was in a wax about the boys whistling and one of the old women had got drunk and taken her room without asking and she said Act or no Act she begged to give notice which she couldn't stick by me for sleeping on a couch was a taste of what prison would be like and which going to bed under such circumstances was nothing but a Empty Pomp!

PASTICHE

A.M.A.

The New Age, November 21, 1912

DESPAIR

"HAVE you heard from Langford lately?"

"Langford! Don't you know? He was killed at Loos[1] last month."

"Loos! Then he must have been in the same fight as my son! I suppose I didn't notice the other names."

"Gorringe went down, too, and Hoad and Repton."

"Repton? No, I don't know Repton. Hoad's father was an acquaintance of mine, and Gorringe, of course, I knew through Willie. I knew he was killed, but it was after Willie. He was a fine head—could beat me hollow on Aztec remains. The Aztecs are gone, and we shall be gone."

"Cheer up. We have a lot to do yet. Think of modern science! We shan't go snuff out like the Aztecs."

"The Aztecs knew things and were modern in their day. They are all gone. My son used to chaff me about the Aztecs, my lad—I can see him now chaffing Gorringe and me. They are both dead. And Langford! Langford, too! He was a crack on...but what's

---

[1] The Battle of Loos took place in September, 1915. British casualties in the battle approached 60,000.

the use? He's as dead as Caesar himself. They'll be all strangers in the army soon. Good-bye, Williams. I suppose you don't know anything about that other friend of Willie's, young Thorpe ?"

"Er—oh; Thorpe? Yes, Thorpe—he's all right."

"I heard he was missing. Thank God, someone's alive! Good-bye."

Williams: Poor old Gray, he's done. I couldn't tell him about Thorpe. But confound his Aztecs! They were savages...But Caesar... and Napoleon too...Fancy Thorpe...it does make a—a vacancy...

NUMBNESS

Dear Mrs. Hatch,—Do you know I cannot remember whether I answered your last letter or not. I have been so busy. My husband was wounded in the head while attacking in Egypt, but am glad to say he is now quite better. I think I told you he is in the —'s. They finished in Egypt a month ago and arrived in France two weeks since. I was hoping with all my heart he would get some leave, but no sign of any yet! The —'s were sent to the trenches at once, and he went in last week. I do want to see him so much! How are you?...If only this war would cease and give us back those we love! It is...

Good-bye!

Yours,

Annie Smithson.

———◆———

Dear Kit,—Thanks for yours...Did I tell you, of course I didn't, that Ben and I have quite decided to get married after the war? He is in Flanders now, having been drafted on from Egypt. It is...

Lovingly,

Edie.

———◆———

My dear Amy,—My poor Claude is almost deaf from an obus.[2] I expected to have him home, but alas! no leave yet. He is much better, he writes, these last days and is returning to the trenches shortly. I wish it were all over and our sons back home! Poor young Clarke, one of Claude's school-friends, was killed. I shall be very relieved to have Claude safely back. It is…

Yours affectionately,

Marion.

APATHY

"What is the price of this hat?"

"Twenty-five shillings, madam. The osprey is real."

"I don't think one ought to wear ospreys during the war. Show me something simple and all black, not crape, of course, I'm not in mourning, thank God; something with a silk crown and fine straw brim. That one; yes, this will do. Yes—P.O.D. Good morning…Let us go on to Selfridge's, Winifred. We can lunch there, and I want to telephone to Mrs. Foster. She has lost her husband—isn't this war awful?—and I'm almost an old friend of hers, so I'm going down to dine with her this evening. I want to know if anyone else will be there—if so, I shan't go. I shouldn't feel easy if she were alone, but there's no need to go if she has someone else. She's very cheerful, considering, but one even gets used to being a widow. One gets used to everything. There's a woman with an osprey! I wonder if they are being worn after all? Look at these skirts; there must be six yards in them. I don't intend to buy another single thing this summer. What does it matter what one wears in a time like this! Mrs. Foster had just got a new outfit. I helped her choose most. And now she has had

---

[2] An artillery shell.

to dye it all! I'm starving. I'll telephone after lunch. How strange to lunch and dine and all that while this awful...

CANT

Poetic: Civilisation, thou diest on the battlefield! See there the duke's son giving his last cup of cold water to the cook's son. When men drink the cup of blood together they awaken to brotherhood. O rich reward of pain, arousing man to...

Prosaic: And after this world-wide cataclysm, progress will leap forward. Capital and Labour, the allied troops of commerce, will unite on the field of peace, shoulder to shoulder, against Prussian greed. Without one drop of bloodshed we, the Allies, in unity, can put it out of Germany's power over again to attack us. Shoulder to shoulder...

COURAGE

The patrol now out of sight and hearing, his terror returns. For a few minutes he dare not even slacken his attitude of attention. On a sudden he vomits, almost too suddenly to lean forward. The effect is a certain steadiness. His head feels less insanely stiff. But the sounds begin again, the rustlings, the cracklings, the thuddings. His heart thumps, and he mistakes its beat for a muffled footfall. He stares over the wet grass of the ditch bank, in a hollow off which he is placed, and up the rise. He commands the rise with his rifle: any rifle over the rise equally commands his head. Before they could get at him, he would hear the crack of other rifles, those of the outposts.

"What a coward I am!" he thinks, and his mind hurries on— "What an amount of energy I am using up in fear. This is my own energy. I could use the same energy to be courageous. It is mine. I have got all this force, and it's being wasted."

His breath takes full, and his heart rises above his knees and comes back into place as if mechanically. He listens. His mouth and nostrils no longer start open, but close, while his ears are at work. His eyes, half-shut, visualise each stirring object, leaves, twig, rolling stone. He practises, as it were, at standing well over his terror.

Soon he observes that, by interlacing two branches of bush on the bank, he may pass for part of the foliage without in the least obscuring his own view of the horizon.

IMPRESSIONS OF PARIS

IMPRESSIONS DE PARIS

Alice Morning

In April 1914, Hastings moved to Paris. Although her relationship with The New Age *editor A.R. Orage had soured, and she no longer worked as the paper's literary editor, she continued to write for it. Beginning on May 21, 1914, and continuing weekly for the next ten issues, Hastings, as "Alice Morning," published a column titled "Impressions de Paris," which combined travelogue with arts and cultural criticism. On July 30, she appears to have felt exasperated with the whole project, and concluded her brief essay with the declaration, "no more impressions."*

The New Age, May 21, 1914

WHEN THE TRAIN had fairly moved, I regretted not to have kissed the dear in spite of the world, which was a fat man, a thin woman, and a middling-sized one. "Don't forget to send us your impressions!" he sang out, and I waved. There was a lovely valley in Kent where I thought I would return for life until I reflected that my train was thundering past the foot of it. They wanted a franc for an apple at Calais! Next time I shall bring a bottle of milk or a thermos of tea, which would be even more serviceable, and some cakes and some apples at a penny each, instead a penny a bite. I would have given away the last two bites to have got out of my Dames Seules compartment, of which the door stuck fast, wide open, and the fenêtre would not shut, but the other carriages were full while I freezed in solitude.

Amiens is where the soldiers come from. I must send him that petit billet to say that my aunt forbade me to take tea with le militaire! Nobody else could have got that window shut! But, my word, all that is quite true about these impressionable French. It is the more amazing that their chairs should be designed for Calvinists. Shall I ever need to despair, since a sleepless night, twelve hours' travelling, and assaults and robberies all along the line leave me the most ravishing person ever seen, seductrice in fifteen minutes of the very tulip of his regiment, aetat twenty-three, and false by everything but the teeniest blink to the mistress I implored him to remember? I shall send all my children to the Lyceé, where they will learn to be so agreeable and to know all about whatever one happens to be reading and about the new movements in art and music. They will understand about customs and baggage, and how to emerge speckless from a combat with a dirty window. They shall go to France, every man Jack of them, and then, when it is forbidden to talk about anything but the landscape, they will invent a historiette of the passing château and fall into a reverie in the middle of it. My horrid aunt will frizzle in blazes hereafter for her prudish existence.

The Paris cocher beats his horse. I should have remembered this; yet the gods do not punish the wicked, for he got away with fifty centimes too much. Jacob's wife had given me the wrong address of the Englishwoman in Paris, so I dined alone at the Duc, which was packed with English, and I talked to a woman who had been to school with my pet aversion and asked me about many bores. I fear that I must have been a bore in one of my past lives, I am so often bothered by bores. An awful French one pinched me at déjeuner. But first—that garçon who heard me murmuring English damns over the ménu, and, taking the situation, intelligently suggested Roast Beef at ten o'clock of the morning! "It is not a bad country," the Bore was saying for the tenth time. "These are not bad people altogether, Messieurs les Anglais—but they are detractors of all the earth. Moi, I have made only a little proposition of an excursion to a lady not young, not beautiful, not rich—and there followed a great scandal." "Ah, monsieur," I said, "we run our Empire on just this tongue-waggery. We rule the earth, we govern our masses by permitting them to say what they please. Our nobles are not such fools as to snip off the tongues of the canaille. We oblige ourselves to suffer this that not in the least incommodes us and makes resigned the others. I, for instance, recently left London a grand example. Last week, I was drunk only three times. On but one occasion did any slight violence occur. A knife and a broken glass found their billets, but, I assure you on my salvation, only skin-deep! Believe me, monsieur, the world made this four times drunk, and the total loss of an ear! I am not a violent woman, monsieur! I could not have done it even in my cups! I will never believe that the G. B. S. ear was more than pierced!" I sank into a glowering reverie over my wrongs. At least, I reflected, while he paid his bill—whatever my dear friends in London may be saying about me, they will scarcely beat this—which that bore will publish all over the Mont.

You can buy thin envelopes in Mont Parnasse, but not thin notepaper. It has never been dreamed of. It costs too much. The papetiere told me so.

You might as well live in a grand hotel in Paris as in a mouse-hole. The two are about the same price, all considered.

Something is always happening in Paris. I have found out that the street I used to take two trams to get to is round the corner. It was yesterday when I wanted to go to Cook's, and I was being tossed from side to side of the Boulevarde by excited persons all directing me wrongly—at least, some of them must have been wrong—when a giant Anglaise rushed up and commanded me in a fashion to make me weep for our high schools: "There—over there—where that lady in blue is—light blue—it's no use waiting here—they'll only stop at the proper places." She was all wrong, this figure of a grenadier, and so presently I wandered back to the thing in the middle of the road. Looking miserably at all the names to be seen, I spotted my roundabout cul-de-sac right close by. I was so pleased that I found the right 'bus a minute after!

I wonder if one has a different accent for policemen and other polite persons from what one uses to savages. I scored, though, over the clerk at the bureau. "Iss betterr you spik Ingleesh?" he suggested. I wasn't going to stand this! " Look here," I said, in unmistakable Saxon, "I prefer the scrunch of my French to the squeak of your English. J'ai l'honneur de vous dire que si vous ne pouvez pas me trouver une chambre plus tranquille je...!"[1] However, tit for tat—he always pretends now that he can't understand me over the telephone, and sends up the waiter every blessed time to ask what I want! I suppose it's because I wear sandals. I'll try him with heels and hobble skirt.

I suppose the Tuileries and things are still in Paris; Madame Sarah Bernhardt certainly is. I suppose one ought to see as much as one can, but what if you don't want to? I have seen the French children. They are adorable! A little duck passed me by the Madeleine and held up one finger. I laughed and winked, and when we both looked back she came running to ask me to go to the dancing! The governess told me she was five, but she looked too enchanted, I think, ever to have been ordinarily born. And they're all gay and graceful, even the gamins.

Inadvertently I became possessed of "Le Journal" instead of the "Les Debats." "Good God," I groaned, "so this has gone the way of all Press—advertisements sneaking in as literary matter!" Then I saw, and rushed back for the right paper. Ah, what a wit of a journal! I even found its anti-Socialism seductive so long as I read. I just caught sight of myself in the glass with that face of a malicious, delicious cut which La Simone is making popular. How horrid!

---

[1] "I have the pleasure of telling you that if you cannot find me a quieter room I...!"

The New Age, July 2, 1914

FOR THE LAST TWO WEEKS I have lost my cigarette-holder, and I've only had one impression. Yesterday a delightful Roumanian rendered it to me, and so I feel lively enough to record an English feminine opinion of these impressions, brought also yesterday by word of mouth. It appears that I air the few French words I've picked up, and that's all there is to it. Clever creature! Presently I'll go Baedekking.[2] One says here that not to have Baedekked once in all these weeks argues the commencement of a great career, but my explanation is that one's tenth hundred custom-house produces an aversion for its city. Sometimes I think I can see in my face an impression of all the steps I've mounted to inspect marvels. I mounted the other day to be shown some Picassos and Rousseaus at a private show. I couldn't abide them, and sat down to read Paul Fort in a magazine that lay comfortably on a table by an armchair. I couldn't abide him either, went to sleep, and waked up to find everybody gone, and nobody outside seemed ever to have heard of the street I live in. I was bouleversée (see Tauchnitz —overthrown, upset) for ten minutes until my friends came racing back just as I had found a gendarme. No! I can't say there is much to it, but what the devil! It's all there is! I didn't like the Picassos, and, if I did, I could not, I suppose, presume to say more than the artists I went with: "Superbe! Magnifique! Oui! Très joli!"

A friend brought me reams of London scandal yesterday. People seem to be leading terrible lives nowadays. I shan't be able to speak to crowds of people when I get back. What a comfort! But that's all there is to it, sweet lady! Paris—I mean my three streets and a cafe—has a very especial kind of scandal. People don't report on each other's physiological frailties—they try to attack the spirit,

---

[2] Baedeker is a publisher of guidebooks for tourists.

like my deep critic. Mention whomsoever you may, someone will tell you that he is "finished." At one moment or another I have heard everyone pronounced finished, from Picasso to my friend the poor poet who has not very well begun. To escape being finished in Mont Parnasse, the only way is never to begin really, but to get the description serieux. (Tr. serious, sweet lady!) Serieux is a "boss" epithet in Paris. To me it looks like dominos and tufts of beard and beer and inattention to anything except the next person to say how-go-you to and well, what are you doing now? "Ah, a merchant has bought one of my things! He is en voyage at this moment, but when he returns—h'm, a-ha!" These merchants seem to go to Jericho and farther amazing frequent.

On the day the Ribot Cabinet fell,[3] after which everything was just as ever, the "Figaro," which smashed about like the "Saturday Review" in a wax, announcing the end of all order, had a literary supplement with twelve more or less original contributions, tales and studies and poems and criticisms, and not a single advertisement on this supplement. Voilà du bon goût, messieurs les Anglais![4] All advertisement was relegated to the ordinary issue. You do not see in Paris, either, many advertisements on the walls. The most frequent is: Advertisements forbidden! The modern Hun, the Harmsworth,[5] has not yet got much of a foothold here. No doubt, he comes, and the cheap and sky-scraping builder is his advance-guard.

If I stayed in Paris, I should discover that snobbery is not insular. They have the English of it, but it's equally French. Le snob! The particular sort of snob I have met here is what visits the studios of promising artists. It is often, deliriously often, a Continental prince or princess, damn dull, that regards the works with neither love nor aversion, but it has heard that this young

---

[3] June 13, 1914, when Alexandre Ribot was dismissed as Prime Minister.
[4] "Now that's good taste, Englishmen!"
[5] Alfred Harmsworth, British tabloid publisher and owner of the *Daily Mail* and *Daily Mirror*.

man goes to arrive! It never buys, this Snob; it patronises in a fashion at once to infuriate and to give prestige. What a horrible metiér! to be—Some women are talking very good French. "Why did you hide yourself this morning? Were you ashamed?" "Yes." "You had reason—you believe well, you had reason! But that arrives to everybody! Don't get red! And how goes the little husband?" It's impossible for an Englishwoman not to laugh in Paris. The naiveté is as azure and Pagan as the sky! But I was saying what a metiér to be at once the Caliph and Maecenas, to destroy the work while patronising the artist! My comparison doesn't quite hang. True, the snob usually, like Omar, is in the pay of America, and only a masterpiece has a chance of being overlooked, but that isn't all there is to it—the snobs somehow manage to kill the artist, that beats anything Omar ever did. A great friend of mine who fished about ces gens artistes (these artistic chaps: Tauchnitz) sold a picture last week for 800 francs. The same evening I saw him in company with a Nut, next day he had a new hat, to-day he promised me a bouquet, and on Sunday I shall send it to his funeral, certain!

I like not myself ces gens artistes. Though they are so spick and span always, yet in a room they do seem a litter about the place, like the gold bands off cigars. Besides, they're spiteful. One has his studio opposite mine, which I've found by the way—no trees, only ivy and roses, but lovely old red tiles and air and blue sky—and I asked him if he minded the piano. No; loved it! And he has revenged himself by singing all the evening in just the sort of trained voice I don't like.

The New Age, July 9, 1914

I FELL among la jeunesse dorée[6] the other evening. My Roumanian, who I find is a Russian, but it's all the same to me, invited me with a thousand lying assurances. He never said a

---

[6] The gilded youth.

word about all that red carpet and old oak more than Waring's and Wardour Street together ever dreamed of.[7] But he did say I could leave at once if I were bored—it was a little soirée à la Montparnasse. It wasn't anything of the kind, and I couldn't leave when I wanted to, which was five minutes after I arrived; I had to wait a good half-hour until he had sung. I must say it was nearly worth it. It was miles away from my spot, somewhere awfully gorgeous. Well, waiters and other things opened the door, and in a second I knew I should suffocate. But there was one lark. A crowd of English of the nuttish genre were annoyed to see that I saw them (they were in all sorts of quaint demi-rig-ups) trying to be awfully in everything in face of a nude and foul-mouthed female dancer. I left after with a final scowl at the preposterous oak, and the host said he was desolated. I heard that within an hour everyone was fast asleep. Bah! But there comes a real fête here soon, the fourteenth of July. If God spares me, I shall amuse myself, for they tell me that there run three days of carnival and not an arrest all through Paris; the gendarmes themselves lead the dancing. But, anyway, these Paris police are men of the world. I heard one reason a monsieur out of a situation which would have required three bobbies and a magistrate to deal with in London. It is all this kind of mental elasticity which makes one feel more civilised here than at home, and in spite of the primitive plumbing.

I'm afraid the destinies are trying to thwart my preference for the simple and penniless. Yesterday, I was lured again among the carpets, to correct, if possible, my impressions of the pictures of Rousseau, not to mention Chinese carvings, and the fattest pug I ever saw who guards nine Rousseaus. It's no use, though, I find Rousseau bourgeois, sentimental and rusé. I behaved myself very badly. The large painting was there of Picasso, a well-dressed Colossus with a palette apparently looking for something left to paint amidst a toyshop world of signal-posts and bridges and aeroplanes all clean as enamelled pins. And there was the picture

---

[7] Waring's was a London furniture retailer; Wardour Street in London had many furniture stores.

of Rousseau's kindred stiffly arranged like a Victorian family photograph out on the grass in scandalous rejection of the verities, everyone of 'em a standing fib in its best clothes. But Rousseau's portrait of himself with Ma Rousseau nearly killed me! Outside was a big cemetery, and I went and pretended to look at it for fear I should simply bust. They are both in black, hair, moustaches, clothes and all, and rigidly holding hands over some little trees that look like the flora of the Strand Hotel, and a country background superbly painted. It is a tricky contrast, and I can't think why all the grocers don't rush to get done like that. They do not, however. But the great touch! The two heads, etherealised up in the sky, each in a little white heavenly cloud, Pa's moustache gone a bit grey, and Ma sanctified by a life of Sundays in black. The artist does paint (sometimes) a country scene that you would forget it wasn't real except for some rotten little ruse of a square man or a dog à la Gamage, or a tree apparently trimmed with giant ears of corn instead of branches! But perhaps I didn't regard it in the right spirit, since I found never quite the true thing anywhere. It's no good challenging myself to say what the true thing is in art. You see it when it's there, and you don't see it when it's not there. I don't know why I get dragged about Paris to look at Rousseaus, and now it is cold again, and I've made thousands of promises to go everywhere when it grew cool, thinking it never would. Ah, by the way, Mr. Walter Sickert-whom-I-adore's compliments to women painters will not wash with me![8] All examined, they only amount to a favourable comparison with some young men crack-pots, but you know no man can pay us a compliment that will really wash at the expense of his own sex. I wonder if the lady-painters were taken in! I expect they were. But Mr. Sickert can say anything he likes for all

---

[8] Walter Sickert, painter, had written in the June 25, 1914 *New Age* a review of the London Salon of the Allied Artists' Association. He took to task the young male painters whose "yelling and gesticulating" he found less compelling than the "modest flowers of a reasonable and serviceable art tended and brought to perfection by women."

I mind about the truth of femininics; when he is en train, he reads well in Paris. I wonder what he would say about the Rousseaus? O bother Rousseau! But it is difficult to drop him for the moment. What beats me is when, for instance, an unsentimental artist like Modigliani says, Oui, très joli, about him. One of Modigliani's stone heads was on a table below the painting of Picasso, and the contrast between the true thing and the true-to-life thing nearly split me. I would like to buy one of those heads, but I'm sure they cost pounds to make, and the Italian is liable to give you anything you look interested in. No wonder he is the spoiled child of the quarter, enfant sometimes-terrible but always forgiven—half Paris is in morally illegal possession of his designs. "Nothing's lost!" he says, and bang goes another drawing for twopence or nothing, while he dreams off to some cafe to borrow a franc for some more paper! It's all very New Agey, and, like us, he will have, as an art-dealer said to me, "a very good remember." They say here that he will do no more of these questionless, immobile heads, as his designs begin to set the immobile amidst the mobile. He is a very beautiful person to look at, when he is shaven, about twenty-eight, I should think, always either laughing or quarrelling à la Rotonde, which is a furious tongue-duel umpired by a shrug that never forgets the coffee. If he only hadn't said thingamy was très joli, I would have left off without remarking that he horrifies some English friends of mine whose flat overlooks his studio by tubbing at two hour intervals in the garden, and occasionally lighting all up after midnight apparently as an aid to sculpturing Babel. Speaking about studios, mine is a duck with two rooms and real running water and gas and crowds of chests of drawers and wardrobes, and only sixty-five francs a month. Anyone will know how cheap that is for Montparnasse. I've inspected the whole quarter and seen nothing near it under a hundred and fifty furnished. You've jolly well got to pig if you want to live cheaply here. I call lack of plumbing piggery, which it is! My concierge is also a duck, and everything's very joyful except a large rat which is a shocking thief.

IMPRESSIONS OF PARIS

Alice Morning

As the July 30, 1914 edition of The New Age *was most likely headed off to the printer, and Hastings had indicated the end of her "Impressions de Paris," the world changed. On July 28, Austria-Hungary declared war on Serbia, and by August 4, all of the major powers of Europe were at war. On August 13, Hastings (still as Alice Morning) began a new column, now titled "Impressions of Paris," which she continued writing nearly every week until November 1915. The essays remain diaristic and personal, and she still documents arts and culture, but they also become a chronicle of the wartime challenges faced by ordinary Parisians.*

The New Age, August 13, 1914

I BEGIN to fill my diary again. All is war now and art is under worse than lock and key. I shall stay if the Prefect of Police is persuadable, though there is no more salt to be had in my district. I have some sardines, some bad rice, and sixteen eggs against the siege. There was an intense moment in Paris after Juarés was slaughtered.[1] The politicians acquired a style in their anxiety. The note issued to the workmen was a clean document, simple,

---

[1] Jean Juarès, French socialist leader and anti-war activist, had been assassinated on July 31, 1914.

truthful. We all wondered what would happen on Saturday when the gendarmes were about, some carrying revolvers in the hand. But it was too clear how much the Government resented the assassination at such an hour for the people to quarrel about it. Out in the streets last night I heard cries against La Caillaux,[2] but nothing about Juarés. The gendarmes, so far, have nothing to do here but arrest any drunken canaille, and laugh and applaud the processions manifesting in favour of the war. They broke up the anti-war meeting with no trouble, simply running the men off the spot, beating a few. You wouldn't wonder if you could see the frenzied faces laughing for war. The men are bright as birds, though most of the women are crying. I thought all the Germans were gone, but I saw two within a few streets of each other being battered for saying Vive Allemagne! Courageous, too courageous! "It is not the moment for that!" as a gendarme remarked to me.

There will be no trouble here with the workmen. Scarcely a sign of civil disorder is to be seen and what exists is only in a few low cafés where the men one will need to be afraid of sing and dance among vile women. Thousands of young men promenade with flags, chanting, some with faces horribly alive. The crowd outside "Le Matin"[3] is stimulated every half hour with some such spectacle. At each block something happens and yet all in a similar rhythm—a solitary soldier passes mounted, loaded with arms and forage, or a squad of brass helmets ride by, or a reservist with father or friend drags his bundle along. A crowd at a corner surrounded an Austrian student, anxiously but bravely enough endeavouring to quieten two midinettes, pinch-faced dwarfs,

---

[2] Henriette Caillaux, wife of French politician Joseph Caillaux, had been put on trial for the murder of *Le Figaro* editor Gaston Calmette, whom she had killed when he threatened to publish love letters written between Henriette and Joseph while he was still married to his first wife. On July 28, 1914, Henriette was found not guilty on the grounds that she had committed a crime of passion.

[3] A French daily newspaper with nationalist political leanings.

yelling at him: "A Berlin!" "Tu t'excite trop, ma gosse," he said to one of them. "Thou wishest to excite everybody." He got away. His fine thin French no doubt helped him.

Money is a little easier. I managed to change a fifty-franc note yesterday after three days' vain flourishing of it. But prices of things are ruinous. My femme de chambre, who seems to live on potatoes, is in tears, and tells me the most fearsome histories of the Commune. "Oh, Madame, I was twelve years old. Oui, my father was killed. We ate bread made of straw. One couldn't eat it, and one ate it all the same. I was twelve years. I sat all night with a blanket in the queue waiting for a little crust of bread, un petit bout, not enough for one and we were six! But that will not come again. Oh no; it's impossible. There were people who ate rats, twenty francs for a rat. Rats! If you had seen that, Madame, you would have thought it shameful. I would have preferred to die." It is not reassuring, but I stay all the same. I was a bit unnerved by a rumour that no Americans will be allowed to stay, and I was counting on some of these, my friends. But the rumours are endless. One hears now of a supreme effort to be made to-day by the pacifists around the coffin of Juarés. "L'Humanité"[4] waves away the antiquated idea of revenging Juarés by the executing of his fanatical murderer, and asks for nothing less than peace. This will scarcely be. When Juarés is buried, there will be not a straw of conflict between the Government and the people. No National Guilds for France, I am afraid! The most alarming sounds come from all quarters, but they are nothing, I think, but echoes of the general roar—striking off from walls and other objects. Outside, nothing is isolated like that; there is community of voice and movement. The moulder down in the court, an Italian, who is too old to serve, yet practises constantly with an ancient rifle. "Wait! when I am ten days older, I shall not be too old," he says. The

---

[4] French communist newspaper founded by Juarès.

furniture-minder, quite a nice man up to yesterday, has become intolerable, dressed in his best suit and flinging monosyllables at everybody—he is called! "Ah, thou also!" he said to his dog, apparently preferring to talk to the cur—"thou hast caught a rat?" I feel out of things, with no possibility of suddenly hating my German friends. It is all a bad business. The French mothers speak with terror of the cruel Germans, and one can well believe to hear the echo of their fear from the other side of the frontier.

———•———

It is Wednesday, the fourth day of mobilisation here, and the last possible for making your declaration and getting a permit to stay. And I'm at home and haven't got mine and it's four of the afternoon. But I positively can't do any more in the matter! I started out at least three hours ago to get it all nicely settled, and when I got there I saw a crowd and tacked myself on to the end of it and read, and presently I found out it was the police station, and the crowd was all the relations of the people who pillaged the German milkshops the other day. So I went on to the right place, or what ought to have been the right place, only they'd moved it to the other extreme end of the district. And when I got there, it wasn't there either after I'd answered ever so much and told them I hadn't got any of the things they wanted. Not being a foreigner one doesn't dream of them! So at last they said it wasn't there and I went on, and off a stall I bought three pounds of plums to make jam, quite forgetting the business, and there were at least a hundred people waiting, and I was the very last in the queue. And when the plums began to come through I couldn't bear any more, so I came home, and now a terrific thunderstorm has broken; I never saw such hail and rain, and if I never go back you're all witnesses that I've tried! The very last straw is that I can't make the jam, which would be as good as meat to me, because there isn't a quarter of a pound of sugar left in the district. I called at every shop on the way. They're all conspicuously labelled, "Maison essentiellement française," for fear of the pillagers who have been making a profitable merit of sacking and destroying firms suspected of being German. However, it is unlikely there will be any more of that as the order is to shoot robbers on sight. Prices, which rose for the first day or so, have come down hurriedly as a result of the infuriated women's attacks on scandalous profiteers. Things are no dearer now than ordinarily. No wonder these French matrons won't even discuss the vote. Their horror of being had in any way seems to give them an extra instinct, a faculty of fixing the attention on what is attainable, which almost resembles reason. After a night and day of suspense, shocks and tears, everyone is now busy making and mending and toiling off on foot to all ends of Paris with bundles for the reservists. Only a couple of metro and tram-lines are in running, no 'buses. They all went off down the boulevards yesterday with the drivers in uniform. Strings of horses go by, all kinds. I passed a string of wildly curvetting hunters yesterday by the Eiffel Tower. One has to look out for oneself now. There are constantly slight accidents and collisions; at least, I only see the slight ones. Almost all the shops are shuttered, there are no men left to shop-keep. Provisions are sold in the big stores by women to the queues, with a gendarme directing, but many of the small shops have closed down, sold out. It seems to me like closing day in London with men uniformed rather like our postmen all over the place, but the change is great for the Parisians. All the cafés are closed at eight o'clock and only men go abroad. The fever of the first day has settled into an especial kind of seriousness which we English are little likely to experience. It contains the difference between attack and defence, the explanation of every Frenchman's instant suppression of his private opinions, and obedience to the first hint of the military. They are fighting for the land. The sense of this has gone out of our blood. My first feeling was something very near contempt of the wage-slave crowds that behaved so harmoniously under police and military. I apologise for myself. Even though the challenge to war may be entirely diplomatic and financial, the stake belongs to the people who will do the fighting; and they know it. Afterwards, we shall see again.

People discuss the fragility of the sense of honour and the "thin crust" of civilisation, declared everywhere crumbled by the Germans. One is dumb-foundered to hear the coolest reflections upon the case that some or other Power may go Hohenzollern[5] and try to rush the planet. The Germans I have seen here since the beginning of mobilisation (they are mostly away under guard now) displayed nothing of this fury, no, not even underneath— where you can see best. Their feeling and manner for the most part indicated bewildered horror and dignity. An acquaintance of mine departed to make her declaration in a fashion to make one ache, full of tears, yet not a drop falling. In contrast with this serious life, are for us others the hundred and one petty and humorous botherations of a state of siege. At the Commissariat (where my declaration is still to be made! I'd forgotten!) a young American girl of something under eighteen lamented—"What an upset of all my Plans. It's too stupid!" Well, I must go again.

Been! No papers! Consul! He lives the other side of Paris! Damn!

Oh, dear, what a time I've had. There was a long, young, red gentleman who looked as if he had just had a tub. I was melting after standing for eight or nine stations in a jammed-full metro carriage; and this tactless thing haunted me so that in two minutes I felt in a nettle-bed. I said I hadn't any papers. "No papers of any kind!" He looked at me as though I had done something to bring about the general state of affairs. "I have my bank-book, though it

---

[5] The royal dynasty of the German Empire (from 1871-1918) and Prussia (from 1415-1918).

isn't signed, and I've brought some copies of a journal I write for, there's my name." I think he threw a glance at it, I won't swear to this! It offended me horribly. He called another man who glanced politely at the bank-book, and asked if I hadn't any letters. "Oh, of course, I have private letters." "Have you one from the editor of this journal?" "Yes." "Will you allow me to see the heading?" And I had to say: "It is not written on official paper!!!" Everything was very suspicious, and I ought to have been amused, but I was nettly. They agreed with each other to let me have some document and then the young, long man said, "Three francs fifty." I had only brought out two francs altogether. Three francs fifty! It is a sum these days! I said I hadn't got it. "I'll keep the papers if you care to go and get the money." And suddenly I wondered what humiliations I might have to support in case I should come to my last three francs fifty. "I shan't give it," I said, and walked out. So, as I mean to go on not giving it…! No, no, why even the grocers refrain in these days from demanding a deposit on their bottles and jars. The British Consulate can fish for its three francs fifty. Americans here are not being asked for money on their papers. But I'll pack this off quick in case they send a regiment after me.

The New Age, October 8, 1914

THE concierges of Paris pretend to believe that this war will be over before the October term! The unamusing discovery that my own term here is up next Friday instead of twenty days hence set me wondering whether I liked the place as much as ever, and I do and I don't. It will cost close on ten francs a week to keep it even half warm! So I started off to see what was to be had. Nothing! Will you believe it, with Paris half-empty, no concierge has anything to let. I can't get at all the mystery, but certainly one reason for hundreds of places being unavailable is that they are full of the furnitures of absentee German and Austrian tenants—which sticks may by luck and lapse of time come round to the ladies of the gate, or, if not the sticks, a fat tip for looking after them. Germans tipped like Americans in Paris, and have in consequence a solid footing of that sort with the concierge class to whom no French, Russian or English need apply until the others are served. A second reason why one cannot find a new place is that most of these concierges, whom one is obliged to ring up every time one enters or leaves a house after ten o'clock, now snore comfortably all night long for lack of tenants, and the small fee they would get for letting a furnished apartment is nothing to their fat pockets. My concierge, though a very, very prudent soul, is quite a grande dame compared with the usual run; by the way, her father, a typically honest cobbler, is too fond of his last ever to have got as far as La Sainte Chapelle after thirty years in Paris! I suppose I shall be found here at the last trump. It rained, it rained, it rained, and I wanted to play on the piano a strain that had been ringing in my head all day, only I had a notion that it might be the Austrian national hymn! I wouldn't venture to risk so much here, but Weber's last waltz didn't seem beyond the pale, although it brought to my memory an unhappy German whom I helped over the border just before he became my Enemy, poor little man.

I shall go miserable for the rest of this incarnation. I went into a shop and bought some steak and it wasn't steak but cheval! I haven't the heart to put it in English. The tragedy came out when I brought in a second lot and gave it to my woman to cook. She warned me, two days too late, always to look for the sign above butchers' shops. Oh, dear, how irreparable it is to eat things! I do feel ill about it, quite disgraced. I thought it was a funny-looking meat, but meat is odd. A crowd of cannibals we are! To brace myself up a little, I went and had my hair singed. The monsieur coiffeur attended me in a garment which was not quite long enough to hide a pair of scarlet trousers! He was a warrior, just in for an afternoon from the Paris garrison. "Twenty and two of our family are at the front," he informed me, "and so far we have not lost one." It is extraordinary luck, for almost everyone seems to have lost at least a distant relative. The pantaloons and circumstance of war put it below his dignity to bother me to buy any pomade or the other unwanted truck hairdressers always try and send you forth with. I came out unfleeced except for my hair-ends.

————— ◆ —————

To my portion, of all people, it falleth to find myself in Paris without a sou. I say of all people because it doesn't seem at all fair. Destiny is quite absurdly wrong if it thinks I deserve any such adventure, and I refuse to take the affair otherwise than as a practical joke which the Laws of the Universe will very soon inquire into. However, here I am, having lived on milk and stale bread since Monday, and this is Wednesday and no sign of a letter from London! Wow! Facile are the stages of coming down from your last two francs to one, and then to not a centime. A person borrows one of the two francs, and then you buy a packet of cigarettes, and then you have exactly thirty-five centimes left, equivalent of threepence-halfpenny. You lay out a penny on bread. Fortunately, your laitierè goes on unsuspiciously leaving the milk, so for the first morning you don't worry—people can live on milk ! Being the sort that would rather swindle than beg or borrow, but not having any ideas ready how to set about the swindling, you cast a mental eye around your acquaintance. You can't discover, for your part, the least personal claim on any of those who have money. You decide for the honour of Angleterre not to ask anyway. Suddenly you think your neck looks dirty. It probably isn't, but not to come down in the world with too great a rush, you wash it again before going out. You have still twenty-five cents, as it were, having heroically bought a vingt-cinq stamp so as to be sure of dispatching your article. On Tuesday, you get unbearably bored, with the studio and decide to go out. Where? There isn't anywhere. You can't go to the cafes. Yes, you can. The Dome is a post-office. You can go and post your letter. Perhaps something will turn up. It does. You meet a pensioner. He cannot be expected to believe that England is ruined even for the moment. The poor soul smiles resignedly as if to say: "So you, too, have come to the end of your patience with me." The letter posted, you walk importantly towards out of sight of the boulevard. Suddenly your coat becomes heavy, your weakest eye hurts, and the wind cracks the skin on your face. Home, home, home! Nothing is changed inside. How might it have—with the key in your pocket! Old tummy is simply howling. Mustn't give it anything in that state. You wait a while and then gnaw up a crust in huge chunks. Agonising results in five minutes. Then you spot a tin of peas. The thing has stuck despised on the shelf so long that it never occurred to you to eat it. Now it occurs. I hate tinned peas. I hate them mortally now. The very last cigarette! Break it in half! Be prudent! The concierge comes to tell you that someone has invited you to dinner on Wednesday evening. Empty news! It is too late. You will be dead before then. You remember a lot of people you like but haven't written to since the war began. Well, it's no use writing now, however much you might want to. If you did write you couldn't post the letters! You think of the old farm where you used to live, the cows—oh, cows, don't mention cows, they mean milk! How nice a cup of tea would be. There isn't any tea.

By ill-luck, no one comes visiting. On Wednesday morning, still blank of the postman, you decide that if you do happen to live long enough for that dinner the best thing about it will be the conversation. The idea of solid food is becoming sickening. A glass of champagne would be acceptable. You think of the bottle you gave away to a frail somebody, last week, and feel inclined to ask the heavens if they don't think they ought to reward you now. You would clinch the bargain for one small ordinary glassful. Oh dear, but it's really no joke. I feel awfully flat, and I don't know a soul who would be absolutely expected to give me any money. Anyway, I shall not try it. It is only a question of a day or two for me, and the Lord do as much to me again if ever I turn a deaf ear even to the adder in distress.

Dear, dear, all that is very much in the swaggering style of a hungry heroine. If I had only read yesterday, as late to-day, Arnold's notes on Joubert, how much more restrained I might have appeared. But I will not be a hypocrite and render my reflections as though the beautiful Literature, that one can live by, had not been necessary to make me forget or control unconsciously the tiresome blood flowing unequably through my body. What a power in style that, like a medicament, can cool a fever of the head and restore physical balance.

In this case I will not say what I intended to about Mr. William Crooks' performance in the matter of "God Save the King."[6] Relinquishing adjectives, I will merely remark that, if he had forced things like that in any school, he would have had to walk home under the teacher's apron. I should think every man in the Commons must have longed to kick the little—no, I won't say it!

Joy be! My letter arrived this evening! My friend who invited me to dinner had just been in long enough to explain that it was an economic concern arranged by some artists, and to hear and wave away my declaration of penury, when the concierge came up with the letter. I opened it, and instantly charged upon her with the billet, demanding a loan of ten francs on pain of withdrawing our troops. Then we went off to dinner. The thing is in a big studio, and people had begun when we got there. I knew several. We reckoned up the nationalities, and this is how we ran: Swedish girl, Belgian girl, Japanese boy, Russian woman (owner of the studio), Canadian woman, Czech girl, Italian, Spaniard, Argentine man, me, a Finn—and then it began Russian girl again, ending with the cook, a Swiss painter. Dinner of soup, meat, fruit, and tea or coffee costs fifty centimes (fivepence), sixpence if you smoke. The cook hopes to keep it going all through the winter.

---

[6] On September 18, 1914, Labour Party MP William "Will" Crooks led the House of Commons in singing the national anthem.

There is no beer or wine, of course; things are too serious; but a good deal of "atmosphere," and you can pay in advance and even have credit as long as possible. Let us hope it can be kept up.

The New Age, January 21, 1915

ACROWD of perfectly honest people seem to be converting themselves to Christianism! By all signs, this included, a wave of hysteria is passing over non-combatants. Paris is, of course, a city of sighs at present. Out of dozens of women you will scarcely find one smiling. Foreigners are being goaded mad by the state of siege. Montparnasse, a foreign quarter, is entirely mad. I find this word recurring in my impressions. The illicit sale of cocaine and hashisch must be something enormous. Fortunately for me drugs have not the least attraction; but one begins to be afraid to take ordinary cheerful liquors. One's head isn't what it used to be! If you like people and find them beginning to drug, nothing avails short of threatening them with the police. I know a charming girl who is going to pieces with hashisch, which is sold for twopence the pill! One feels that one ought to turn informer. In contrast to all these new devotees, the old hands are renouncing the vice. It makes a grand passion rather absurd to be shared by every little person ; and every spot is more or less of a hashisch den now. So you find people of a certain prodding morale searching for a discipline of some kind; and Christianism serves the immediate purpose. I suppose Christianism always did serve the immediate purpose, being ready-made. I happen to be the kind of creature that naturally writes out moral injunctions from all sorts of pagans and heathens and nails them up on the wall. I can only just comprehend the need of a rational person to support himself by a discipline not of his own arrangement.

The world is old, happily. It is probably just entering on its period of cold youth. That is, the eternal youth of the artist. But "cold" is such a chill word in English. The artist's state is dispassionate, even, balanced, everything that implies feeling controlled. The generations to come after this astonishing buffet of war upon a mechanical civilisation should produce a youth unlikely to become food for powder—not mad, not melancholy—no timid, blustering student youth making a jolly row all night and, in the morning, a sad poem about his row. It should be a youth stark awake to the power of man and the indifference of gods both to his melancholy and to his jolly row. Man will have found himself unheard in his shoutings to the god's—these whom all the combatants are now adjuring to be helpful. Man will have found himself left in the trenches with nothing but a murderous, decapitating, limb-shattering mitrailleuse[7] of his own invention between him and his human fellow. The new youth of the world will not likely be Christian. It will be instructed, undeceivable, cold to religious frenzy as to all other feminine freaks of the solar plexus. Hyperborean, perhaps, is the description for this cold youth, la jeunesse froide. The enemies in art will be the dry, cold men, arid men who have nothing to do with the hyperborean, men who arrive at the ice, who, perhaps, even surpass it, but who never see the Pole even when they find it, knowing no more than to plant the flag of their special cult, and get back.

I almost was about to believe, while reading his article "Affirmations," that Mr. Ezra Pound was about to wake up.[8] But he sank quietly deeper on the pillow in his final paragraph, which is only an affirmation that he is a hopeless cultist. Bless my heart, Vortices and the Quattrocento! Why drag in physics?

---

[7] Machine gun.

[8] Pound published a series of seven essays titled "Affirmations" in *The New Age* from January 7 to February 25, 1915. Here, Hastings responds specifically to "Affirmations II—Vorticism," which appeared on January 14.

"Is it," asks Mr. Pound, "that nature can, in fact, only produce a certain number of vortices? That the Quattrocento shines out because the vortices of power coincided with the vortices of creative energy?" It is all fiddling with terms; and creative energy is power. Were there no vortices in nature before the Quattrocento? Yes; and whirlpools, and surges, and Charybdis, and the wheel of Ixion, whereon was bound the poor diable who embraced a cloud thinking it was Juno. I knew a woman once who had decided that everything went in spirals: and, by the way, she played little tricks on you with magic candles and perfumes that arose out of nowhere. The state of things in Art which Mr. Pound deplores is somewhat due to just such florid, pedantic, obscurantist critics as himself—Ixions whom not even an introduction to the almighty gods can clear of pretension. The main reason for the helplessness of artists during the past century is the subjection of all other ideas to the idea of commercial prosperity. Arnold prewarned us of our mad-house while we were preparing to enter it, but while, already, Art was left solitary in its temple. All that the cultists continue to obscure he explained in the "Function of Criticism," which is to be had for a shilling in "Everyman." The passage begins: "The exercise of the creative power is not at all epochs and under all conditions possible"; and it concludes: "For the creation of a master-work two powers must concur, the power of the man and the power of the moment; the creative power has, for its happy exercise, appointed elements, and these elements are not in its own control."

Why obscure and limit this word power in connection with a term like vortex, of physical meaning? All these phenomena in passing for the true critic! Arnold probably understood what is a vortex! It is no more comparable than any other working of fluid with the working of creative power that is possible in such epochs and under such conditions as Arnold describes with the simplicity of perfect understanding in this wonderful essay.

My French reading this week has been mainly of the Letters of Voltaire, some of which come startlingly upon the present crazy state of things aesthetic: the letter to Thieriot for instance. "You have passed your first youth, you will become old and infirm; there is what you must reflect upon…What will become of you when you shall be old and abandoned? Will it be any consolation for you to say to yourself—'I have drunk in good company'? Reflect that the bottles of a feast are afterwards thrown in a corner…"

Writing when the French were dozing before the Revolution as they dozed for so long afterwards, and before we English had become commercialists, Voltaire addresses authoritatively someone whom he seems to disguise as a "head clerk," and who had taken the notion to render a service to Art: "We put, every year, more industry and more invention into our tobacco-shops and our other baubles than the English have needed in order to make themselves masters of the seas, to make steam, and to calculate the rays of the sun. The ancient Romans raised prodigies of architecture for the gladiatorial combats; and we have not known for a century past how to build a hall fit to contain the master-pieces of the human mind!"

They changed something of all that in France after Voltaire; and we in England changed also, so much the worse for us! But the French forgot Voltaire. You should see the "Magic City" on the banks of the Seine, the shop called "La Samaritaine," to know how base may become even a people that produced a Voltaire.[9]

One does little else now save read. I read the "Nation" where there is an article tragically entitled "A Ghastly Dew," in reference to the hurling of bombs from aeroplanes. A more light-minded article would be hard to find. Science, biology and the fine thoughts of poets are tumbled up in one subject with the "sporty" stylisms

---

[9] Magic City was a Paris amusement park built by Ernest Cognacq, owner of the La Samaritaine department store.

of some "car" journal or other. "When shall women vote? When men fly," but the oracle was delivered in despair. "O for the wings of a dove!" cried the Psalmist longing for rest in the wilderness, but there was no answer to his entreaty. The writer, afraid to say what he thinks somewhere in his muddled head about the "ghastly dew," and almost as much afraid to think what he says about the glorious exploits of the latest destructive toy, quotes two or three more poets on the horrors of warfare, and ends in a tone of spiritual insight— "From the beginning mankind has devoted his most splendid arts and inventions to the slaughter of his fellows, and it is not laws or restrictions that will prevent him. Something different from external law is needed for that." Well, yes. And perhaps one would not do so badly to commence by learning a little respect for the poets. But really one finds almost nothing in the Press but what traduces even the war spirit. Worse than the vulgar vaunting of a kind which you never hear from soldiers themselves, is the constant photographing of prisoners of war. I have here the "Mirror" with a frontispiece of some German officer just captured, furious with shame and rage. He is glaring, or seems to be, at the swine of a snapshotter: the French guards both have their heads certainly deliberately lowered.

The latest "Times" scare here is about sixteen—or is it sixty?— Zeppelins that started to bombard England, but somehow never arrived. I read the other day, on "Times" authority, that we cannot induce the upper classes of England to take any pride in becoming officers. We can get men, but not officers, and why doesn't the Government do something—and so on; all, of course, calculated to make a very poor impression here.

I haven't been to any theatres or things, though many are now giving matinees and some few evening performances. I dislike matinees, and also the idea of coming home at night through the gloomy, patrolled streets. My greengrocer provided me with a little comedy. "Ho!" he was saying, "I shall eat my dinner even if we have quarrelled." He was trying to serve five people at once, so I gathered that madame had revolted. "She is fat!" he declared.

"She has a great haunch. Quinze centimes—merci, madame! Look at her!" She wasn't there, so we couldn't look. "It is not to say that I want respect for her if I implore her not to get fat, is it? Une livre de mandarines—vingt-cinq centimes—elles sont biens belles—merci, madame. Truly, life is bitter. All the same, I shall dine, look you. She will understand me better to-morrow. Bonsoir, madame, merci!"

How dreadful to be a poet and praised by your contemporaries! Mr. Upton Sinclair gives one a horrid notion of Mr. George Sterling.[10] It looks silly to be found hewing chestnut trees. Poets don't hew trees for any reason. Then all that about being passionately fond of the sea from the shore side and glorifying in colour: Trite! Fancy a poet without a sense of colour! And that stern sense of the dignity of his art! I don't care one scrap for my part to know whether Mr. Sterling is a Socialist or ever walked in front of the Standard Oil Company; and as for his sense of colour and his stern sense of the dignity of his art, his two sonnets tell us sufficient of the first, and his contributions to "Munsey's" and the "Smart Set" of the second. It really needs a critic to appreciate a poet at his proper value. Mr. Sinclair's unbalanced eulogy has very nearly victimised its object.

Re-reading these impressions, a thing one never ought to do and which I almost never do, I want to suppress the whole. Of course, I am interested to hear that thingamy is a Socialist; but I didn't want to hear it in that particular fashion, a sort of advertisement! I'm glad he stamped about in front of Rockefeller's—but the thing should have been said altogether differently from the way it was, the which was a theatrical way and full of the most unfeeling cliches: Ah! me voila! Mr. Sinclair's letter has not a thought in it from beginning to end, it is in syntax and phrase a lump of "smart" unthought, unfelt cliché. I have counted twenty of the most facile phrases a man might write.

---

[10] Sinclair had written a letter to *The New Age* praising the poet George Sterling that appeared on January 7, 1915.

And the simple-lifer "stunts" of being found rurally occupied, of course set me ready to believe the worst of Mr. Sterling.

The New Age, July 22, 1915

A LADY'S stray remarks about war, although primarily of no account, seem to arouse at least curiosity, if somewhat menacing curiosity. "Why do you not write what you mean? Do you believe in war, or not? I defy anyone to say from your writings."

I defy them myself. I am sure that it matters nothing whether or no I believe in war. My correspondent cannot be asking me whether I believe in war for war's sake! She must mean the present war. Anyway, if we limit the question to this, I may be able to leave off shilly-shallying. Even thus it is not so easy. The fact is that while I am glad enough to be protected from the Germans, I really do not think I would have sacrificed the life of a single man for that. But really, I have accepted my situation. War is a man's affair, and I don't come in at all in the matter of believing in it or not. My part is to nurse or sew or cheer or shut up. If I break out into an opinion it must be blamed on to a false education, or the double-edged licence of the modern woman, or, at its best, the contact with men on service. I mostly cheer because the soldiers are all so cheerful. If I weep, this is because I have just seen a friend weeping. If I rave, this is because (usually) someone who has very little or no more than I have to do with the war has written something treacherous to the side which I am born on. When a someone like Lord Kitchener[11] makes a Prussian speech, I want to rave, but, instead, I become dejected and think about going to the dogs with the country, but in the rapidest and most cheerful possible way. It is hateful to think of the civil trouble

---

[11] Herbert Kitchener, 1st Earl of Kitchener, prominent in British military recruiting efforts.

there may yet be in forming an English army under threat, and miserable to contemplate the resentful and inglorious deaths of those who may be driven in under a kind of stigma, as would be the case of conscripted regiments in England. A cousin of mine, wounded, has disappeared; very few of ours die in their beds: but I should feel like dying dismally in mine if the two or three dreamier youngsters who are at home were ingloriously killed under English compulsion. It beats me how any woman can cry up the idea of conscription; such cannot know what they are doing. My opinion is that the women of men under conscription are sharply divided (saving wonderful exceptions) into those that grow hard or even wicked, and those that grow for ever old with grief, sometimes unconquerable, sometimes heroically hidden. It is a great deal simpler to bear up for a man who goes way for an ideal than for one who is torn away. And all possible activity granted, bearing-up is the average woman's business in war-time. Conscription is a side of war which women's influence may conceivably touch. It is no sane work for women in any way to urge men towards war!

Apart, of course, from what seems to us the unnecessariness of war, the horrors of it are exaggerated in women's minds. By sea and land the world over, death is everywhere at every moment and in every terrible form. The horrors of war do not stop men from making it; and therein is contained the only judgment possible. The combatants, wounded, go again with confounding cheerfulness! I begin to think that I don't understand much about men. It is probably my infamous old age creeping on. Ten years ago or so, my young brother went through a war and brought home a beautifully written log-book, with photographs taken in action and developed and pasted in between whiles. I took it all for granted then, like the sixpence he remembered which I owed him. Now, I think him a terrible kind of animal to shoot an enemy and snapshot him.

Lord Kitchener drove me to reading a fashionable novel by way of starting off to the desperate dogs. It was "Tante," by Miss

Anna Sidgwick.[12] I recollect that the public loved this book when it came out. I think it is exceptionally nasty. Women novelists notoriously cannot keep their hands from destroying—this one destroys with much gall. The heroine, a great woman pianist, is set up only to be debased below any other character in the book. I say "character," but the word is lenient, for what traits and speeches are natural are such general ones as may be observed, en voyage, of a thousand people. The Genius is thoroughly mal-treated in words, but one feels only a half-amused indignation as though someone had vexedly scratched at her photograph on some programme. She is selected for introduction at an age when her glory may reasonably be thought to be passing. As for her person, she could not be called "fat," but a certain "redundancy could not be denied." A conventional young very successful lawyer, who is to marry her ward, is shown in feeling that something is lacking in the musical performance which charms the rest of the world; he wonderfully catches her out in several small unamiabilities: this is the false romantic method—to forewarn us that the Genius and he will come to blows, and that he will win out. It is a fixed idea with the timid of this earth that we instinctively dislike people who are to injure us: the fact is not so. A party of the lawyer's bourgeois friends is arranged to show that the Wonder does not overwhelm everybody—a neat flattery this of the library public. An old domestic person, a true-hearted, strong-tongued American, has only to tell an unsupported story to set everyone believing the worst of the Great Woman. Finally the grand creature is literally exposed throwing herself at a sleek, blase little married Brixton man who does not want her. Could the most malicious desire more? The Goddess is absolutely down. Miss Sidgwick lets us even see the servants carrying in Mercedes (quite a lot of people call her just Mercedes) by her head and feet.

---

[12] Anne Douglas Sedgwick, mispelled here, was a popular British novelist, and published *Tante* to great acclaim in 1912.

Nobody else in the book who matters at all is let off unspoiled. Even the ward, Karen, is given only a loving dog's intelligence and is only allowed to take her husband, the lawyer, as an undeniable make-shift after the wicked woman genius has been found out human, all-too-human. The clever London lady, Mrs. Forrester, is shown grossly tactless just where her experience should have served her. The spinster adorer, Eleanor, is as catty as fable would like to have her. Mrs. Tallie, the American, only bears with Mercedes—who, be it noted, bears with her in spite of her taletelling (this looks like an oversight)—because otherwise she would he absolutely desolate. In fact, ladies, there is not a soul we need envy, unless it were the lawyer's sister, who is so happily made that she never notices that her husband is a "dull fellow!"

To my mind it is a thoroughly lowering book. It would be a sign of some beginnings of feminine culture if similarly spiteful novels were generally ostracised instead of being generally carried in intimate baggage to the lovely spots where we go to refresh our delicate bodies and minds.

The dear old "Athenaeum" gives my Impressions a kind of a compliment, if I liked to take it that way. It begins a review of Mr. Rowland Strong's book, "The Diary of an English Resident in France," by saying—"The writer of this extremely vivid and unabashed diary deals out his experiences and impressions 'en gros et en détail,' without fear or favour; indeed with the exception of 'Alice Morning' in THE NEW AGE he is unequalled for outspokenness: 'Alice Morning,' moreover, wastes much of her superfluous—not to say essential—energy in various NEW AGE by-paths." I reply, as prettily as possible, that I cannot admit anything as wasted which is really NEW AGE and offered to NEW AGE readers; and that I hope the "Athenaeum" may never give up wandering down its own by-paths because I insist on having it principally for these. I'm afraid I am all by-paths. I don't like crowds, that is why. I like anonymities, and countries where there are no pass-ports, and people I have never seen who leave me little bits of money, and babies who go to everybody like sunrays, and nuns who always take to me as, I suppose, never possibly any kind of a competitor, and the sixpenny gallery where you can move if your neighbour gossips, and lighthearted bohemians who say such inhuman things about one that even the truth isn't believed. I like my old mother who never believes anything against me unless she can put it down to my "funny way of life," and grandpapa. I like the "Athenaeum," which will not mind a bit about my bypaths fifty years hence, will even, perhaps, raise an eyebrow at the indiscretion of some publisher's editor who may suppress them. Not that I would bother to go down all of them twice myself! But then, one doesn't write Impressions with an eye on Immortality. Lord! I do ramble, and I haven't said a word about Paris.

MEMOIRS

MADAME SIX

Anonymous

Madame Six *was published serially in* The Straight-Thinker, *a short-lived paper Hastings edited in 1932 and 1933. According to her biographer Stephen Gray, the published text is incomplete and the full text has been lost.*[1] Madame Six *is based on a long convalescence Hastings spent in a French women's hospital. This volume includes installments which appeared in* The Straight-Thinker *1.1 and 1.4.*

The Straight-Thinker, January 23, 1932

(An Englishwoman in a French Hospital, October, 1920.)

AWAKENING: in a hospital bed screened around in a corner beside a vast window white-washed for a yard up, and then, trees just as I love them, half-stripped and still, against a faint October dawn. I have been here a month. It is half-past six. Every physical need satisfied. No pain. Head, as always, clear as a bell. A fat packet of books and reviews from Ezra Pound. A pen full of ink, and plenty of paper.

---

[1] Stephen Gray, *Beatrice Hastings: A Literary Life* (New York: Viking, 2004): 469.

And, as if suddenly, after several years' neglect of everybody, I begin wondering what has become of So-and-So, and hoping that Un Tel[2] may not be dead, or that Chose may be.

I have changed in five years—since I left off publishing, not writing. Carl Bechofer Roberts, who was through from Russia, belauded me as the only person he had ever seen grow younger, but that is not what I was going to write—vanity rushed me away. The change I personally notice is my present philosophical acceptance of what used to make me indignant. I don't see myself now demanding someone to fasten Machin, or another of the Mud Group of poets to the gate of a criminal lunatic asylum. I reflect—"The fellow has barely enough talent to control his emotional fluid, but since he has enough—proof, that he writes instead of raping and slaying—he cannot legally be tied up. Further, in the absence of literary critics who know anything about style, let alone physiology, pathology, and psychology, there is no way of limiting his evil influence on a weak-minded public which, after all, may go to the deuce for all I care."

————•————

Barbellion's[3] remarks on reviewers, matter formerly for wrath, only just touched me. Said I—"Don't I know their eye for eye and cutlet for cutlet tactics? Haven't I had some? Aren't I a boycotted martyr for having once had principles and dared to call a spade a spade, not to say a damn bad writer and a block-head and a log-roller and so on? Most of which assertions I solemnly declare shall be republished in volume form, since my critical articles besides being scientifically and aesthetically well-founded, are good reading. The names of the criticised might be left out without suppressing anything but their one and only chance of immortality.

---

[2] A play on "Untel," French for "so-and-so."
[3] W.N.P. Barbellion, English diarist, author of *The Journal of a Disappointed Man* (1919).

—•—

What a style in Zinoviev's address to the German syndicalists! What a challenge to the so-called artists whose Stuff peters out in translation! Take almost any translated address by Lenin—the same thing is seen, the style coming clear through.

But I'm in bed, awakening only. Why so much energetic admiration all at once?

I'm in love, that's why, God help me! If I am to face the world with these nerves of mine all uncovered as they seem to be! For I am sensuously in love with the trees, with the sky, with October. This is a kind of madness, and I shall not know how to control it. Certain Facts have always touched me to the tragic kinds of passion, pity, terror, despair—but my tears have never fallen for natural beauty. I enjoyed it robustly. Now…I know that I am ill, and going into the winter. I suppose that I yearn after these things because I may see them no more. I would bind them to me like a lover by some service, some bribe which they may only take by sharing their life with me. And they cannot be bribed, any more than lover's love. Finish with this. I become unintelligible even to myself. God help me, natheless, if my old magic disguise is going to quit me. I am not now capable of making a new one.

Disguise! Anything to hide the stranger...

Disguised! Rather! Many roles, and all doubled.

A Bacchante with Martha's apron on. Maecenas in a red tie. Messalina coiffed like Mary of Bethlehem.

How many more? As many as I have physionomical expressions, the which, by the way, tire out painters and sculptors. They can't "do" my face. Nothing but a sixpenny snap-shot has ever shown what I am like at any given moment.

Two or three people have suspected me in Paris—Modigliani, Apollinaire, Max Jacob, and two or three others.

Modigliani—always suspicious, always returning to Martha's kitchen, often to find it in possession of the Bacchante, always expecting his welcome down from the Cross, and sometimes getting the hoof from Messalina, scoffing equally at Maecenas and the Comrade and never quite able to walk around either: inspired every day with something about me—"voila, encore une" or "encore un", he would say—I never knew what he meant and was too arrogant to ask. I never posed, just let him "do" me, as he pleased, going about the house. He did the Mary portrait of me in a cafe where I sat thinking what a nuisance he was with his perennial need of more pastels, wondering if I should get my "Impressions of Paris" written in time for the post, hearing, not listening, to his spit as he lowered his eyebrows on the aesthetic canaille who all went to his funeral along with his friends—and next day, beginning to wonder why they had done so, looked around for revenge and advised the world to sell his stuff "while the vogue lasts."[4]

The Straight-Thinker, March 5, 1932

THE three-day-old Madame Un suddenly appeared around my screen, came to say goodbye, by the way of excuse to see what I looked like. She was charming, with the sweetest, most pathetic little apache face and that slightly husky young-crow voice one hears from the Paris gamine. Madame Un was only sixteen and a half, but everybody is called Madame here, old or young, single or married. And, by the way, the girl-mother has nothing to fear; the French respect for "private life" leaves her free to face her troubles without any additional burden from the unco guid.[5] Never once have I heard the slightest attempt to rag one of these filles-mères, several of whom have passed in and out since I have been lying on my back. Madame Un said that she regretted infinitely

---

[4] [Hastings's note] (1925. I say that my own admiration of his talent was strictly limited since I discovered that one thing I had raved over—a stone head—was a copy of some Italian sculpture!)

[5] "Unco guid" refers to someone who is strictly religious. See, for instance, Robert Burns's "Address to the Unco Guid, or the Rigidly Righteous" (1786).

not to have seen more of me and I said that I was desolated to lose her so soon, and then she went off with a "Better health, chere Madame!" People are fond of attributing the easy grace of the French populace to the effect of Catholic training, but this is a wild notion nowadays, if ever it had a basis in reality. Many a priest is a perfect boor and many a nun an utter outsider, the supply coming mainly from the bigoted of the peasant and shopkeeper classes. The grace of the people is certainly due to the Revolution which endowed them all with the liberty to express themselves, and I think that the title of Monsieur or Madame which the Revolution secured for everyone, even a beggar, considerably smooths the way to ease of manner in speaking. In England, no-one knows how to address a stranger; the person who brings it off properly is quite a genius. Thank goodness, here we are all Madame and a number. I once heard English nurses in a public hospital with their "Mrs Er, Mrs What's your name," and a sudden—"Oh—Mrs Thomas!" the lady's name being Tompkins, and am glad they don't do it here. No-one wants their name called out in a crowd at all, let alone upside down. If our populace ever make a revolution, I hope they will all call themselves Sir and Lady, our average way of saying Meddum and Moddum for Madame being decidedly objectionable.

———•———

If I write anything bitter in these pages be sure that either:

1. They are mopping the floor of the ward.
2. I have just submitted to a piqure.
3. The nurse has upset water in my bed.
4. The weekly railway-accident has delayed the milk for my coffee.
5. Mesdames les autres malades are really going on a little too long at a stretch in the narration of their obstetrical exploits.
6. No-one has turned up to see me.

7. Someone has who would smile at seeing me dead.

8. Or, I have forgotten to replenish my stock of sweets, substitute for cigarettes.

———◆———

A sample from the reviews which are demanding "strong criticism". Mr. T. S. Eliot: (italics mine).

> But *what* have I, but *what* have I, my friend,
> To *give* you, what can *you* receive from *me*?
> On*ly* the friendship and the sympa*thy*
> Of *one* about to *reach* her journey's end.[6] (Pom!)

Passing for decasyllabic verse, tis all nought but polka. And almost the whole of "Prufrock" must be scanned like these horrible lines, almost the whole of it!—all but ten lines of pretty good prose.

He criticises too, does Eliot, "Aristotle", says he, "Aristotle, curiously enough, is more purely a poetical critic than Coleridge." There isn't grass enough in the sweet heavens to match the colour of it for a judgment. Impayable, that "curiously enough" in a statement which would need twenty-two academic Internationals not to mention the help of Heaven, to decide.

———◆———

"An author over thirty years has no more curiosity about anonymous visitors." (Marcel Prévost.) This is Writing for provincials. To make such a boast to Paris would be equivalent to having his photograph taken at home in full rig waiting for someone to ring at the bell.

Some foreign princess said to her French aunt, "They laugh at everything in Paris, aunt," I haven't seen anyone laugh, but they

---

[6] From Eliot's "Portrait of a Lady."

do understand just the reverse of what one says—candour being a ridiculous qualité here, politeness demands an amiable scepticism of anything like a plain statement.

———◆———

I return to Browning and that "Commemoration Book"; homage to R. B. It is time to opine that "curiously enough", since Shakespeare there is only Dickens whose work might conceivably be a loss to the Recording Angel. Not rare Ben Jonson not equally rare a hundred other writers but would be less missed than Dickens when it came to wanting a record of the human species. This, by the way, O Foolish Reader, is not to pair off Dickens with Shakespeare; but he follows, and so far there is no-one else in the line.

I am here almost tempted to show why Goethe and Racine and Swift and Tolstoy and Cervantes and all the innumerable rest would be turned down by our Maker if he should ever care to ascertain whether the human creation is staying—as it was meant to—where it was put, human nature being fixed...and not necessarily as bad as it prefers to be. But it would take such a long time, and I don't quite know how long I've got left. I prefer simply to state that "curiously enough" it is so. This lets me get on to point out that the Great Novelists of our day, Meredith, Hardy, Conrad, James and Browning, really a novelist, have written mostly around puppets. (Wait a moment. Don't run away.) Meredith's "gentlemen-animals" with their lady-animals, would be of no use to the Recorder because they are a mode invented by Meredith. Consider: anyone, even a villain, would instantly detect a Meredithian character in, say, a Hardy novel, and vice versa; imagine then, what would not the Recording Angel, in his unspotted innocency, if one or other of these branded flocks of mannikins came parading as Mankind.

I am not insinuating that it is any nobler to be, like Shakespeare and Dickens, of service to the immune gods than, like Meredith, to a certain reading public only asking to be fashionably deluded. I don't know any more what is or is not noble, having suffered too much from both genres and if ever I seem to think I know—this is merely moralistic atavism based on "Honesty is the Best Policy" and so on. No. But, as Nietzsche said (oh, how that recalls old Fabian debating days! Once, G.B.S. going the Shavian one better, got up yawning "as Nietzsche would doubtless have said."), "My taste" happens to be for that kind of literature which, also as it happens, would best serve a divine commission of enquiry into the stability of my species. Men like Browning, Meredith and the rest give themselves the task of enumerating everything they can think of, new and old, and it is all quite amusing but no more informative about Mankind than a catalogue from Gamage or Whiteley which, nevertheless, comprises everything Man has or needs, from a sock to an automobile and bears illustrations of the Man actually wearing the sock and communing with his wife or the chauffeur in the automobile. Nothing being absolute except the fixity of type, the pictorial man in the motor whose evident satisfaction moves Billy de Vere to sing Ta-ra-ra and rush in and buy a car, might be considered as informative about Mankind—quite as much as, and a deal more than, Meredith's man who passed for a bronze statue; which could not move anyone except to doubt; or than his other mannikins in any of their Meredithianly gentlemanly pranks. One cannot imagine these "characters" outside their proper "atmosphere". Try and put Diana Redfern, or whatever her name was, (Crossways) into the "Madding Crowd": she would upset the Hardy waxworks with her Meredithian mots d'esprit and antics.

As for Browning, he had read and learned more than any man except Methusaleh could hope to digest in one existence here below. As a rule he just vomited back what he had swallowed, slightly different, of course, as would only be natural. This simile, an exact one, will offend certain persons. I'll change it, being quite indifferent, and say that Browning wrote down almost exactly what he had read and learned, but in any order which came first, and in the staccato rhythm peculiar to himself—and to the great many like him. This rhythm, which he thought "free" (a common notion) is most often simply bad stock-rhythm. But he finds a thousand liveried lackeys ready to defend him who endowed them with his facility and his blessing on "all instincts immature". Browning's secret was flattery of the failures. See the way the poets in this "commemorative" book repay their awful debt!

I suppose that the rare readable verses were sent by people not realising what company they were in for; still, they ought to have known—probably did know and didn't care—I qui vous parle could not have not cared. But then I think, almost know, that I am a prig.

I am a prig (sick of Browning, want to talk about myself) in more ways than the literary. Had an instance only this morning— for illness does not of course change people's natures. I gazed up from my little white bed curtained off in the corner beside the window over the garden (there's a string of prepositions Vernon Lee would love to adverbialise), gazed into the autumn trees all coloured by the sunshine, and even although I am very ill, I reflected thus-wise: Sure as I am that my Reputation will be systematically and ruthlessly burned at the public stake—nevertheless, I shall continue to scorn, openly if pushed to it, such of my aesthetic compatriots here as I would not abide in London! There are persons who unwarily say that I am a bohemian, and others who unwarily take me for one. I think that I am a prig and being ill in no-wise alters my being. Even, I fancy that I have been really too tolerant, altogether too liberal, towards little persons from London.

I shall correct this when—and if—I get out again.

THE OLD "NEW AGE": ORAGE AND OTHERS

Beatrice Hastings

This is a selection from the opening of Hastings's short 1936 book The Old "New Age." *Hastings wrote the book after her former lover and collaborator A.R. Orage—editor of* The New Age—*died in 1934. In her opinion, obituaries of Orage gave him too much credit for* The New Age, *and ignored the significance of other contributors, most notably herself.*

I.

EXTRACTS from the Introduction to "Incidents in the life of the old *New Age*, 1907 to 1916". A book in preparation, by Beatrice Hastings.[1]

De mortuis nil nisi bonum. Of the dead say nothing but good. The late A. R. Orage improved on this precept, that has had its share in falsifying history. For many years before his own departure, he said nothing at all concerning his deceased colleagues on the old "New Age." Indeed, he pushed circumspection so far as to anticipate the passing-on of some of us who have survived him, and maintained silence as to our

---

[1] This projected work was never published.

very names. Huntly Carter, that indefatigable bee who, besides his own contributions over many years, induced hundreds of home and foreign flowers to give their substance to the "New Age" columns, became a subject for reserve. But the most sacred taboo was applied to me. It was an indecorous wight who ventured to mention to Orage—Beatrice Hastings.

De mortuis nil…

We may, or may not, be pardoned—it will happen according to the company—for expressing our private conviction that there was a definite attempt to brick us up alive.

But, what proof? Even were the result of a course of conduct proved, what proof that the course had been planned and the result intended? And then, what personal gain and promotion to the planner?

Carter tells me that he has a book in hand that will deal with such queries, so I speak herein for myself alone, except in so far as I defend my dead colleagues, J. M. Kennedy and A. E. Randall.

———•———

Among the unintelligent who desire someone's disappearance, simple satisfaction of spite and rage is enough; but no plotter ever yet aimed at the mere downfall of his victim. Although spite is ever the heating passion, with Codlin as with Pecksniff, with Iago et hoc, there is always a cold passion down below.[2] Codlin wreaked his spite on Short as the real, although invisible, showman, but when he whispered that Codlin was the Friend, not Short, he heard the coins already rattling in his pocket and saw himself honoured at the feast and Short out in the cold. Pecksniff not only manoeuvred de bon coeur to embroil the young Chuzzlewit with his friends; he also stole the credit for his design of the grammar-school. Iago plotted

---

[2] Codlin and Pecksniff, Dickens characters.

To get his place and to plume up my will
In double knavery.

This double knavery works so smoothly that it is hard to detect which half works first; but it is certain that a cold passion lives with a man and enters into all his behaviour, whereas spite needs special circumstance to make it active. This double knavery is so difficult to unmask that dramatists and novelists are mostly driven to call in coincidence and confession to make a fairplay ending. The victim is rarely in any sort of position to defend himself, since only the unsuspecting can be victimised, and be his own character good, or even middling, and his brain a busy one, warning will fly past him. So, history, if not fiction, is often the history of successful and glorified plotters. There was only a stage-play slip between the cup and the lip of Iago, and, if he had succeeded, he would have heard as many Evvivas as Mussolini, while forgotten Othello rotted in the earth and Cassio cooled his exiled heels in some Libya. Hitler's June 30th hand finds many of the world's high folk willing to shake it...[3]

But, this is gadding too far to fetch comparisons from the vast political Jungle where real bloodstained plotters can get almost whole nations to part with affectionate worship. I just note that, but for the gift of the gab, neither Hitler nor Mussolini might ever have attracted any attention, and walk soberly back to the small literary jungle. Here, although aspiring Leaders still need to collect their crowd by offering honey (with, of course, opportune threats of vinegar), inconvenient colleagues can be put out of the way by that most discreet of poisons, the Boycott. It is very simple: you just say nothing. The method is not vulgarly to bleed your victim, but to dry up his blood. Such an aspiring leader, with such methods, I assert, was the late A. R. Orage.

---

[3] June 30, 1934, also known as the "Night of the Long Knives," when the Nazis carried out a series of political murders of leaders of opposition parties.

———◆———

And who am I, unknown Beatrice Hastings, to make such an assertion in the teeth of a whole small cosmos that has cried Heil! and Evviva! in every variety of tone?

A woman who knew Orage intimately for six years, between 1907 and 1914, who knew him at least as well as anyone else ever knew.

A sub-editor of the "New Age" who, for all but a few months of those six years, had entire charge of, and responsibility for, the literary direction of the paper, from reading and selection of MSS. to the last detail of spacing and position.

A writer who contributed in a dozen various styles under different pseudonyms and anonymously.

A woman who offended Orage's masculine amour-propre, and for this, was made the victim of a social cabal—that did not matter even to herself—and of a literary boycott that does, or should, matter to every reading person.

There was a famous case in Paris some years ago of an attempt by a well-known author to organise a campaign of boycott against his former *amie* and colleague. Paris laughed—they do these things better in France—and someone crushed the business with untranslatable wit: Mais ce coquin érige en juge littéraire son lingam dépité![4]

But also, the woman was on the spot, knew the ropes and fought like a lioness. I never knew any ropes, was absent when the plot began and for many years after. When I returned, the damage was done. In 1925, Clifford Sharp warned me that Orage had made a cabal against me and that I should find a ring of reviewers and publishers' readers ready to oblige him by

---

[4] "But that rascal raised as a literary judge his disappointed lingam."
A lingam is an abstract representation of Shiva, usually phallic in nature.

boycotting my work if I wished to publish.[5] I was then absorbed in other studies, had no intention of publishing or even of remaining in England; so the warning went past me. But, I had time to find out that those of my old friends and colleagues whom I approached were singularly changed, that once their curiosity to see me was satisfied, they were anxious to drop me and that I was no longer persona grata anywhere. Except Hannan Swaffer, Anna Wickham and Ruth Pitter, who then expressed a scarifying opinion of Orage, but later did *puja*,[6] and Huntly Carter (Kennedy and Randall being dead), no-one so much as invited me to lunch.

A year or so earlier, things might have been different. Orage, having ruined the "New Age", had fled, was considered to have "flopped" forever; but now, he had gone to America, was making name and money on Social Credit and—was expected back to form his circle again in London. How he was hailed may be judged from some of the letters of personal compliment that he published against the usual rule. *Many of the writers were really saluting The Old "New Age"*, but the effect of the whole was an apotheosis of Orage.

II. NOTES

IT IS EASY to see when I began to take the literary direction of the "New Age". For the first time, the paper shows some signs of being edited instead of being merely filled up. I put it without fear to any competent editor in the world.

Until I came in, the "New Age" editorially, was a rag; until I was free to come in entirely, in summer, 1908, there were frequent

---

[5] [Hastings's note] Later, I sent three books to six publishers by same post. They all came back in a week to ten days, evidently rejected at sight by the Readers. One book was "Madame Six". I say quite coolly that a period when "Madame Six" cannot find a publisher is a *literary* period *pour rire*.

[6] An act or ritual of devotion and worship in Hinduism.

issues of rags; and after I "left", it degenerated to a rag again. Not only had Orage no idea how to present what he did print, but he regarded creative work as mere trimmings; at least, this was his refuge from a realisation that he was no artist himself. New writers were waiting, as they always are, the matter was there, but Orage valued neither them nor it. He could see nothing but big names around his own. How he treated correspondents, unless these were big names or protégés of big names, or complimented, may be seen in the early issues; he did not print their letters, but only his own smart retorts! the kind of tin-god's insolence to which he subjected not a few aspirants to "The New English Weekly", that wooden ape of the "New Age" I finally formed.[7] He used poems for filling corners, and made few corners. Except for an occasional story by some known writer, Orage printed practically *no original work*. Before I came in, the young and unknown got no chance. If there are six names, with a quarter of a column to each, and Titterton's stories, I think that will be the full sum. He pshawed when I rescued from a drawer several manuscripts—for he accepted things, this costing him nothing but a smile or one of his famous notes, and a place in a pigeon-hole—and I said that these ought to go in. One was a sketch by Raffalovich (oh yes, malgré Orage's tap on the drum, Dec. 6, 1917) and another a poem by Flint. When I first gave a half-page to someone's poem, there was an hour of protest, and when I decided on Ashley Dukes' first sketch, I was advised to invite in the whole Fabian Nursery and be done with it. But I had a temper not to be trifled with. Soon, I got the correspondence columns really opened, and things began to be lively enough. But the paper only became what I wanted when J. M. Kennedy and A. E. Randall and Huntly Carter settled in and we made a sort of frame that could stand the inevitable fluctuation of outside contributions. What J. M. K. was to the "New Age" will be seen presently.

---

[7] Orage founded *The New English Weekly* in 1932.

So far from having the flair for writers with which he has been credited (at my expense), Orage had less than common judgment. One of the few lively writers on "The New English Weekly" was rejected time after time, until Dr. Oscar Levy wrote to Orage protesting; then the new and unknown man, now with a fair-sized name himself, got his first space.

———•———

In "The New English Weekly", May, 1932, Orage pretended that Katherine Mansfield had "shown" him her first sketch and that he had published it. At that moment, I happened to be in a position to reply publicly. I threw down the glove in my "Straight Thinker Bulletin". This was a four-page sheet that I brought out when I had to abandon the "Straight Thinker" that was virtually killed by Orage's advertisement, a week after I started it, that he was starting a paper "as a revival of the old New Age." My subscriptions stopped, and contributions fell to almost nothing. I had to print serials in full of which I had intended only a synthesis. The "Bulletin" was doing well and even getting advertisements when I fell dangerously ill and was hors de combat for a long time. Well, I gave every detail to prove that Orage had—lied. I informed the public, so far as I could reach it, that every literary manuscript for the "New Age" passed through my hands. Orage did not dare to take up that glove. Neither did he print another "Talk" with K. M. He slunk off in silence. In Paris, New York, Addis Ababa, or any other capital, the comic papers, even, would have obliged him to reply. In London, no-one blinked.

———•———

Among "New Age" contributors who have expressed their gratitude to Orage for giving them a start, few have sung him louder than Mr. Ezra Pound.

In this preliminary pamphlet, I must suppress the detail I shall publish later, so simply say that I had to fight not only

Orage, but the whole office, to get Pound's articles in at all. They were so idiosyncratic that I did not quite trust my own judgment, and I read them out; and everyone howled. However, I put them through. But, Orage scoffed at and belittled Pound in and out of season. On one occasion, Orage, who knew almost no French, but had the self-assurance of a Parolles, said—"I reserve my judgment [on French writers Pound had cited] until he has produced his evidence that any one of them can write good French." Finally, when I wrote, as "T. K. L.", a series of parodies of certain poets introduced by Pound, who took the jousting with tolerable literary manner, Orage, *butting in* with his flat, ponderous pen (and what a flat, ponderous, stilted, maundering, when not coy, conceited and facetious, when not plagiaristic or outright thievish "literary" pen he had, I shall later demonstrate) said, so late as Oct. 1913, nearly two years after Pound's debut: "Mr. Pound's style is a paste of colloquy, slang journalism and pedantry. Of culture, in Nietzsche's sense of the word, it bears no sign."

I put it to anyone outside literary Bedlam (and for the nonce, I put Pound inside it) whether an editor able to do as he pleased would have persisted in publishing a contributor of whom he thought like that? Orage had nothing to do with the publication of these articles, four or five longish series. Orage discovered that Pound's translations interested a great many readers, but he continued to rage. (Note: Pound had to be *paid*.)

———◆———

During all those years, Orage coolly took for, and deliberately attracted to, himself the compliments about the wonderful paper, although editorially he had almost nothing to do; the front pages were fixed, and the manuscripts he dealt with were mostly by old hands and experts whose quality called for no judgment. He allowed new writers to thank him for giving them a start when he rarely saw their work until it was in print. Everyone, without exception, who got a "start" between summer, 1908 and May, 1914 (and even later, for MSS. were sent to me in Paris), owes that start to me and to no-one else. They count by scores, and many of them have "made a name."

And here I invite anyone to count those who got in after I was no longer even consulted about the editing, end of 1915. Just that. Orage, who had not a particle of genius, hated "creative" writers.

———◆———

My present-day friends, accustomed to the push and publicity of this period, find it hard to understand how I could be so disastrously indifferent to claiming my work; how I could go on, year after year, writing anonymously or under pseudonyms that allowed readers to set down my work to other people, mainly to Orage. Puzzle or no (I could explain it with more space; I thought it better for the paper) there it is. I did so. I cared for nothing but the paper, that was my life. I am far from regretting, either, for the work will eventually come back to my door, and I could not have done it if exposed to the publicity I should have had by signing every thing and if it had been known that every new contributor had to reckon with me. I took enormous pains not to be identified. Incidentally, my first contribution to the "New Age" was an unsigned column and a half review of Orage's "Nietzsche in Outline and Aphorism", Nov. 30, 1907, and my last, an article from Paris, signed "Alice Morning", March, 1920. [8]

---

[8] [Hastings's note] This name was inspired by the fortune of a cousin of mine who went as a junior in the "Morning" to the South Pole.

In May, 1914, domestic affairs having become intolerable, I left for a few months' tour in order to make a break. Randall was to take over most of my editorial work, as he understood it well. I think Orage soon displaced him. The war broke out, and I was valuable as Paris correspondent, so I stayed on there, sending weekly "Impressions of Paris" and other articles for over two years.

———◆———

Here, I say that I am not concerned now merely to establish my own claim. It is too late for me to get anything like personal compensation, and my intimate friends would testify how often I have shrugged aside their indignant advice to make a stand. There is a bigger thing at stake. There is the reputation of the "New Age" itself, that is, of the collectivity of contributors who aimed at a high standard in creative and critical thought of all kinds, however some of them may have fallen away since.

I have a certain sensitiveness to the currents running through the literary world (although it seldom serves me personally), and a very particular kind of luck, the journalist's luck—although I was never a journalist in the practical sense of the term—of being on the spot, of meeting the right person, of hearing the significant thing. And I sense that, since the deplorable attempt to pass off "The New English Weekly" as a "revival of the old New Age" and since the publication of "the best of Orage's writings", an opinion is gaining ground that the "New Age" was over-rated. I declare that this is not so. I have been going through the volumes lately, after twenty years, and I am inclined to marvel. We builded even better than we knew, and we were not afflicted with false modesty! There are hundreds of contributions that have no date and never will have any date because they belong to the ray of liberal mind (the real, not the imitation that tolerates even the enemies of liberty) that is as young and as old as humanity itself. I could do an enchanting summary of each month with the story and, the stars agreeable, I will. No, the falling reputation of Orage is not going to drag down the "New Age" with it. I have not, so far, troubled much to defend myself, but I shall trouble on the "New Age" issue.

And, since I am personally inextricably mixed with it, the mettle of my present ideas and ideals should be understood: whoever may have changed from the early days, I have not. I am still the author of "Woman's Worst Enemy, Woman",[9] as well as of "The Maids' Comedy"; I still love the social rebel, and challenge mere man-made laws and hate the Pankhursts, Emmeline and Christabel, who sold the Feminist movement; I am the same crusading, anti-philistine woman I ever was.

Last, but not least, I realise that, without an explanation from me, the future critic could never make sense of the "New Age" story.

---

[9] [Hastings's note] Aldington exploits this title, in one of his books, without naming me. That this silk-fingered, scratch-nailed, sob-stuffing, eaten-brained curate of the feminine soul is accepted by women as a champion shows what enemies to themselves they still are. [Editor: Hastings is likely referring to Richard Aldington's 1933 novel *All Men are Enemies*.]

GALLERY

All images of *The New Age*, courtesy of
the Modernist Journals Project.

All photographs of Beatrice Hastings, courtesy of
the H.P.B. Library in Toronto.

p.161: Amedeo Modigliani, *Madam Pompadour*, 1915.
Oil on canvas, 24 1/16 x 19 3/4 in. The Art Institute of Chicago.

p.164: Amedeo Modigliani, *Beatrice Hastings*, 1914-16.
Graphite and conté crayon on paper, 13 7/8 x 9 1/4 in.
Solomon R. Guggenheim Museum.

p.165: Amedeo Modigliani, *Béatrice (Portrait de Béatrice Hastings)*, 1916.
Oil on canvas, 21 5/8 x 15 3/16 in. The Barnes Foundation.

p.166: Amedeo Modigliani, *Head of a Woman: Portrait of Beatrice Hastings*,
1913-1914. Marble, pedestal of varnished wood, 30 x 8 x 10 2/3 in.
Musee National d'Art Moderne, Centre Georges Pompidou, Paris.

p.167: Amedeo Modigliani, *Béatrice Hastings*, 1915.
Oil on board transferred to panel. Museo del Novecento, Milan.

THE
NEW AGE
A WEEKLY REVIEW OF POLITICS, LITERATURE AND ART.

New Series. Vol. VI. No. 12.   THURSDAY, JAN. 20, 1910.   [Registered at G.P.O. as a Newspaper.]   **THREEPENCE.**

INDIGESTION.

Beatrice Hastings 1918.
(Very ill.)   *Paris.*

NEW PUBLICATIONS issued by the New Age Press, Ltd.

Printed for the Proprietors, The New Age Press Ltd., by A. Bonner, 1, 2, & 3, Church Passage, & 38, Cursitor Street, Chancery Lane. Agents for South Africa and Australia : Gordon & Gotch, London, Melborne, Sydney, Brisbane, Perth (W. Australia), and Cape Town ; and (S. Africa), Central News Agency, Ltd. Business Offices: 12-14, Red Lion Court, Fleet Street, London, E.C. Tel. 6111 Central.

Beatrice Keeling
Dieppe 1924
(very ill.)

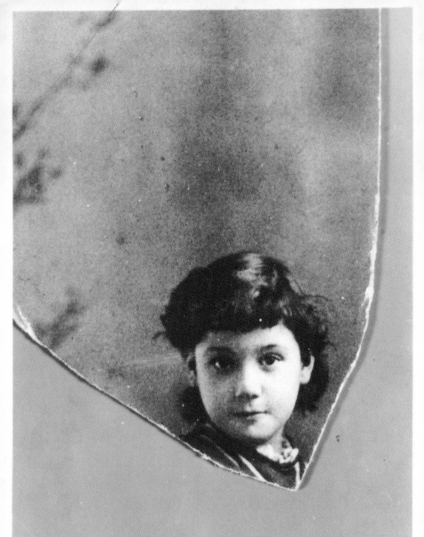

Beatrice Hastings.
7 yrs old. 1886.

Not whipped, but nagged. The Ugly Duckling. Decided to run away & be a Robber Chief.

The wire across, must have been accidental, although it looks so appropriate. Photo was taken in the back garden.

Beatrice Hastings.
19 yrs. 1895. "In full revolt."

ESSAYS ON BEATRICE HASTINGS

BEATRICE HASTINGS'S SPARRING PSEUDONYMS, FEMINISM, AND THE NEW AGE

Carey Snyder

CAREY SNYDER is an associate professor at Ohio University. She is the author of British Fiction and Cross-Cultural Encounters: Ethnographic Modernism from Wells to Woolf *(Palgrave, 2008) and the editor of H.G. Wells's* Ann Veronica *(Broadview 2015). Her articles on British modernism have appeared in a wide array of journals, including* Modern Fiction Studies, Journal of Modern Periodical Studies, *and* College Literature.

From 1907 to 1920, Beatrice Hastings deployed over a dozen pseudonyms in the pages of the socialist weekly *The New Age*, several of them fully-developed personae that she at times pits against one another, literally staging arguments with herself. Hastings evidently saw the periodical as a playful, even emancipatory, realm where she could cast off her flesh-and-blood identity, donning a variety of disguises of different genders, rhetorical styles, and political persuasions. In crafting these myriad identities, Hastings prefigures what Margaret Beetham describes as the allure of Cyberspace to "leave behind our embodied selves, play with gender and sexuality, discard differences of age or physical ability and create virtual communities."[1] Yet though pseudonyms can be used to "rework gender," Beetham shows that such reworking occurs "within constraints not just of material but also of ideological power."[2] Like other virtual identities, Hastings's proliferating pseudonyms were crafted within certain limiting conditions—most significantly, that of working within male-dominated print culture—even as they ingenuously liberated the author from a fixed style or perspective. This essay explores the way that Hastings maneuvered within the masculine culture of *The New Age* as the sole woman among its four core contributors, using pseudonyms creatively to try on a range of feminist and anti-feminist ideas, experiment with different perspectives, and provoke debate.

Edited by A. R. Orage from 1907 to 1922, *The New Age* was a London-based review of politics, arts, and letters with a tradition of fomenting aesthetic and political controversy. It covered topics ranging from women's suffrage and labor issues to the philosophy of Friedrich Nietzsche and Post-Impressionist Art. It also published diverse literary styles, from traditional realism to avant-garde poetry and fiction, frequently subjecting its own contributors to clever parody. According to one contemporary, Hastings held her own in the masculine milieu of *The New Age* "by sheer force of character and volume of production," and her copious copy—signed, anonymous, and pseudonymous—played a central role in inciting controversy.[3]

By writing so much pseudonymously, Hastings risked erasing her work from cultural memory. In her 1936 professional memoir, *The Old "New Age": Orage and Others*, she attempted to salvage her reputation by providing readers with a key to thirteen of her pseudonyms. These ranged from one-offs, like Pagan and G. Whiz, to robust signatures, like her Paris correspondent, Alice Morning (with 108 items to her name), and her satirical persona, T.K.L. (with 45 items).[4] T.K.L.'s rhetorical purpose was so well-defined that Hastings called the act of writing a satire or parody "doing a T.K.L.,"[5] and in 1932, she even staged a dramatic comeback of this pseudonym in her magazine, *The Straight-Thinker*.[6] Despite her belated effort to secure a reputation by unifying this disparate tribe of pseudonyms under one signature, it is only in the past decade that Hastings has begun to find a place in literary history.

The signature "Beatrice Hastings"—itself an assumed name for Emily Alice Haigh—did not appear in *The New Age* until December 30, 1909; instead, the author made her debut in 1908 with the firebrand Beatrice Tina, who courted controversy by celebrating militant suffragism and rejecting motherhood. In consistent circulation for about two years, Tina was remembered by contemporaries decades later, nearly upstaging the author herself.[7] In January 1910, Hastings pit the coolly rational "D. Triformis" against Tina, denouncing militancy and taking aim at leaders of the women's movement. In 1913, Hastings veered in a new direction, engineering two male pseudonyms, Edward Stafford and Sydney Robert West, who verged on caricatures of male chauvinists, yet whose radical, anti-feminist views echoed those Hastings had begun to express under her own name.[8] Focusing on Tina, Triformis, Stafford, and West, this essay endeavors to illuminate the nuanced work that Hastings's pseudonyms did within the spheres of feminist and anti-feminist debate.[9]

Although scholars have emphasized the magazine's "anti-feminist tendencies,"[10] in its first four years *The New Age* was relatively open to discussing feminist topics within its feature articles as well as its letters section, while also offering a platform to anti-feminist and anti-suffragist writers.[11] From May to July 1907, it showcased a series of articles on women's suffrage by "Truculent Teresa" Billington-Greig, who had gained notoriety as one of the first members of the movement to be imprisoned for the cause. From May 1907 to January 1908, British West End leading actress Florence Farr also contributed steadily on women's rights, advocating for the vote and for the legalization of prostitution, and offering bold feminist criticism of the theater. After publishing a "Women's Suffrage Supplement" in February

1911, *The New Age* no longer included pro-feminist and pro-suffrage writings among its features, and the magazine began to overtly position itself "against the vote and against the liberties of women."[12] In August 1911, Orage launched his misogynist column, "Tales for Men Only," and a year later, in a pair of lengthy editorials, he retracted his earlier support for women's suffrage and proclaimed that women, who had been misled by "the dangerous doctrines of Ibsen and Shaw," should return to the domestic sphere.[13] Orage's reactionary remarks prompted Dora Marsden, editor of the newly founded *Freewoman*, to dub *The New Age* "a paper written by men and for men."[14]

While the proliferation of Hastings's distinct voices was unusual, pseudonyms themselves were common in *The New Age*: for instance, J. M. Kennedy published under the tongue-in-cheek alias "S. Verdad" (a Spanish homophone for "it's the truth"), and the fiction writer Arnold Bennett doubled as Jacob Tonson, reviewer and literary critic. Some pseudonyms were open secrets; others, effective disguises; Hastings, in particular, prided herself on evading detection.[15] Partly, pseudonyms served the pragmatic function of swelling the contributors list; partly, they affirmed the socialist value of collective labor.[16] Indeed, Hastings justifies her supposed "disastrous indifference" to claiming her own work by asserting, there was "a bigger thing at stake": "the reputation of the 'New Age.'"[17] Pseudonyms also furnished the author with creative license; she could not have written so boldly or freely, Hastings reports in her memoir, "if exposed to the publicity [she] should have had by signing everything."[18] Above all, Hastings used pseudonyms to try out different voices and perspectives and to promote the journal's combative culture of ideas.

The fiery, pro-militant Tina rose to prominence in June 1908 when Hastings deployed this voice to counter the anti-feminism of Ernest Belfort Bax, a barrister and well-known socialist and anti-feminist author. In his feature article, "Feminism and the Franchise," Bax describes suffragists as a "clamouring," "shrieking," and "ranting sisterhood" whose platform constitutes "anti-man legislation"; far from suffering any "social injustice," Bax asserts, women are a legally "privileged class" who seek suffrage "as a weapon wherewith to carry on a sex-war, with a view to the dominance of the female."[19] In "Woman as State Creditor," Hastings's Tina counters that not only are the legal privileges Bax lists dubious, but they constitute "insulting and contemptuous" repayment for the "odious" degradation of maternity and "the torture of child-birth," which she deems "the ugliest fact in human life."[20] Proclaiming the need for women's economic independence as well as political enfranchisement, Tina concludes with a rousing declaration: "We are prepared to draw up our own terms now, and the fiercer the opposition, the more certain we become of the extent of men's addiction to tyranny. The militant suffragettes have saved us from the last ignominy of the slave—the obligation to give thanks for enfranchisement."[21]

Fashioning men as tyrants and women as slaves, trumpeting suffrage militancy, and construing motherhood as anathema to the independent woman, Tina's remarks were clearly meant to be incendiary. By espousing such maverick feminist views, Hastings's persona succeeded in stirring controversy, which unfolded in the journal's Correspondence section: Fabian writer Edith Nesbit, a self-identified "advanced woman"[22] and mother of six, called Tina's views of motherhood "unholy" and "unnatural," and another reader charged that the "exaggerated Feminism of Beatrice Tina is far more damaging to the Suffragist cause than the anti-Feminism of Belfort Bax"; a third thanked Tina for "articulat[ing] the cry of the 'highly-developed, imaginative woman'" against maternity as the universal law.[23] Thus rather than polarizing the discussion into "pro" vs. "anti" feminist camps, Hastings used this voice to provoke debate *within* "the women's movement," showing it to be far from monolithic.

In the following issue, Hastings devised a one-time pseud-
onym, A Reluctant Suffragette, to more pointedly highlight di-
visions among women: whereas the Tina that routed Bax was
anything but reluctant, this voice only warily joined the defiant
suffragettes who must battle not as much patriarchal men as
"The Other Women": the demurring class of wives and spinsters
who wanted to preserve the status quo.[24] In the next Tina article,
with the ironic title, "The Case of the Anti-Feminists," Hastings
again changed tack, now sarcastically lauding anti-feminists for
"repressing" both their carping wives and their cowering ones,
since both varieties would "tear" independent women like Tina to
"pieces" if they had a chance.[25] As Lucy Delap argues, this "curi-
ous article…must be read to some degree as feminist, establishing
the voice of an independent, creative woman, and mocking male
claims about chivalry [...]. But it was unusual for a 'feminist' voice
to [...] advertise conflict and division among women."[26] Hastings
thus mobilized a range of fictitious identities to "advertise con-
flict" and to test the boundaries of group affiliations.

Hastings also employed this controversy-generating per-
sona for her novella *Whited Sepulchres*, serialized in *The New
Age* from April 29 to June 10, 1909. The narrative centers on the
painful disillusionment of Nan Pearson, a once-artistic youth
with naïve romantic fantasies whose soul is mangled and body
prematurely aged by marriage and motherhood. The implicit
message is that young women should not be allowed to marry
swaddled in such dangerous illusions. Its themes echo those
of Tina's journalism—especially "Woman as State Creditor,"
which we have seen actively unveils the supposed "degrada-
tions" of marriage and motherhood. Nan's mother and married
friends accept wifely and maternal humiliations as their duty
and mock the defiant suffragettes that Tina has so vigorous-
ly defended; they represent the conservative, domestic wom-
en that Hastings derides as A Reluctant Suffragette—a link
Hastings drives home by borrowing an epigraph from "The

Other Woman" for her novella. Recoiling from her brutish husband and eschewing a lover out of fear of scandal, Nan is left a "wreck of womanhood": the minister's wife remarks at the novella's close, "I feel you will become my right hand in the parish," and it is clear that Nan will acquiesce, martyring herself "all in accordance with the rules."

Hastings further exploited Tina's reputation as a maverick and provocateur by expanding her *New Age* writings into a volume entitled *Woman's Worst Enemy: Woman* (1909). Delap observes that "[k]ey feminist ideas were edited out" of essays, such that "Woman as State Creditor," for instance, "no longer [served as] a reply to anti-feminists, but a very open, and consciously controversial discussion of women and maternity."[27] The title underscores the book's polemical intent—implying that women perpetuate their sex's inferior status—but Hastings was evidently frustrated with feminists' failure to engage with her ideas, complaining that *Votes for Women* "would not even mention that it had received a copy" of the book.[28] Judging from her failure to engage interlocutors, Hastings may have pushed the maverick individualism of Tina so far with this publication that it was no longer legible as feminist. Fairly abruptly, Hastings stopped enlisting Tina for feminist debate, using the persona only occasionally over the next year, mostly for poetry, before retiring it completely in May 1910.

Historically, pseudonyms have frequently been used to shield authors from the social and legal repercussions of expressing controversial views;[29] however, the Tina alias did not function in this way. It was more than a pseudonym, serving, uniquely in Hastings's repertoire, as an intermittent public identity: it was as Beatrice Tina that Hastings held a membership in the Fabian society and advertised a room to rent in her flat, for instance.[30] Rather than a shield, Tina seems to have functioned as a radical feminist alter ego. Pseudonymity enabled Hastings not only to shift perspective and voice, but also potentially to reinvent herself—inhabiting and discarding different identities.

Hastings replaced the passionate, polemical, pro-militant Tina with the ultra-rational, sometimes conciliatory, anti-militant voice of D. Triformis as her dominant persona from January to May 1910. (Although Triformis self-identified as female, at least one reader assumed that Triformis was male,[31] a misunderstanding that Hastings would seem to encourage by not specifying this persona's first name.) Readers outside *The New Age* coterie would have no reason to link either persona to the obscure Hastings, whose first signed items in the journal coincided with the emergence of Triformis; yet the archival reader—privy to Hastings's shape-shifting talents perhaps slyly hinted at in the name *tri-formis*—glimpses an apparent reversal in argument and approach. Whereas Tina exalted the methods of the suffragettes, potentially goading women to further acts of violence, Triformis, in a trio of articles opposing militancy, insists that since "peace... is the basis of civilisation," women should seek "serene equality"; and "what humanity needs beyond all things is an understanding between men and women, a mutual tolerance of each other's particular desires."[32] In Tina's oppositional world of male tyrants and female slaves, there had been no room for "mutual tolerance."

Why did Hastings craft a new persona at this juncture? Whether or not the author changed her mind about militancy,[32] Triformis enabled her to "try on" a different perspective without opening Tina up to charges of inconsistency. With nothing like Tina's generic range, the new persona was designed for a narrow rhetorical purpose: to lead a frontal assault on the militant suffrage organization, the Women's Social and Political Union (or W.S.P.U.); its founding members, Emmeline and Christabel Pankhurst; and its organ, *Votes for Women*. Although Tina sowed discord within the feminist movement, she did not wage an all-out war against suffragettes, as Triformis did; this may be because Hasting was not yet willing to alienate this constituency of so-called "advanced women"—a potentially lucrative market for Tina's book, which was still being actively plugged in *The New*

Age.[34] Disdaining militant methods, Hastings's new persona embraced the language of chivalry that Tina mocked, chastising the "fanatical pioneers" who resist every "concession" and "revolt" from "protection," turning away from the male sympathizer's metaphorical "hand holding out graces, favours and immunities."[35] Hastings thus enlisted Triformis to do what Tina, with her so-called "exaggerated feminism," could never do: flout the supposed fanaticism of her fellow suffragettes and the feminist press.

One male reader accused Triformis of underestimating the "wrongs of women" and unfairly condemning her "heroic sisters"; another characterized her as overly "academic," doubting whether her appeal to cool reason would be efficacious given that the masses respond to emotion, as the suffragettes realized.[36] These responses notwithstanding, the Triformis persona was not as effective as Tina in firing up debate, and in apparent frustration, Hastings had Triformis ramp up the discourse, dismissing the whole program of the militants as "stupidity" and the hymns and speeches of the W.S.P.U. as nothing but, "in plain English, rant."[37] Still, the suffragettes did not take up the gauntlet. In mock bafflement over the silence, Triformis wondered "whether, perhaps, the WSPU had never heard of THE NEW AGE" or whether they simply did not suppose her "worth arguing with."[38] One correspondent provided a plausible explanation for Triformis's cool reception: "she has attacked, one after the other, the motives and methods of the ordinary Suffragist—no doubt she has some new and original ones of her own which may prove useful if made public."[39] Triformis's failure to engage other women in debate may speak to the limitations of a directly combative approach. It may also speak to Triformis's failure to cohere as a unified voice: amidst her blasting of other positions, it was hard to tell where Triformis (let alone Hastings) stood.

To compensate for Triformis's lack of conversational partners, Hastings audaciously manufactured conflict by staging a duel between her two feminist personae. In an article arguing that women are only oppressed by self-forged manacles, Triformis objects, "When Miss Beatrice Tina wrote: 'The militant suffragettes have saved us from the last ignominy of the slave— the obligation to give thanks for enfranchisement,' she penned, though in a spirited style, one of the most foolish fancies of the average thoughtless woman."[40] This strange, comical moment of staged self-division—where one persona calls the other a fool— can be read as Hastings's own revisionism, or simply her rehearsal of a different point of view. As Tina, she rhetorically emphasized the need for militancy by deeming women slaves; now, as the cooler-tempered Triformis, Hastings points out the hyperbole of the earlier remark. Hastings gets the fun of both the original passionate flourish and the rational rebuke, pulling the puppet strings to act out both sides of a spirited argument.

This staged attack provided a segue for Hastings not only to bring Tina back in the correspondence section of the next issue, but also to step forward and claim her as an alias—for she signs the letter "Beatrice (Tina) Hastings." Hastings revives Tina, after nearly a year of silence on feminist issues, ostensibly to defend her against the charge of folly, but actually to air what is now legible as Hastings's personal grievance against the W.S.P.U. for boycotting her book. Avowing that she has "learned a good deal from D. Triformis," Hastings maintains the fiction that Triformis is a "real" identity, pretending to smart from the blow of her accusation: "she need not have thrust me out as merely a foolish woman."[41] By signing this letter, Hastings outs herself to the wider reading public as the firebrand Tina, now embracing the role of provocateur, with both its rhetorical successes and its social notoriety. With bravado, she boasts that it is a "distinction to be the only woman in England who does not want a family," complaining that for speaking unpopular truths she has been "cast out by advanced women." Still an obscure name in *The New Age*, Hastings thus embraces Tina's maverick identity as her new trademark.

Yet if Hastings adopted Tina as her own through the performative device of her signature, she also stifled this persona, for she washed her hands of the, albeit complicated, feminist views that Tina represented—renouncing not just a virtual identity, but a public one. Tina and Triformis were rendered obsolete as Hastings veered toward misogyny in her signed writings, even as she embodied the economic and professional freedoms and the powerful voice for which the women's movement was fighting. While the shift toward anti-feminism remains somewhat puzzling, it can be seen in part as extending a radical individualism, apparent across Hastings's writings, which made her wary of the women's movement as such.[42] A turning point was her campaign against the White Slave Traffic Bill, supported by many suffragists, which legalized the flogging of pimps and procurers. Regarding white slavery (e.g. forced prostitution) as a fiction and flogging as barbaric, Hastings became, as Delap notes, "highly skeptical of the influence of women in public life."[43]

In 1913, increasingly regarding women as vindictive, irrational, and unfit for politics, Hastings enlisted the first of her two male avatars, Edward Stafford, to support her anti-flogging campaign. In one of Hastings's many instances of veiled self-citation, her persona Stafford commends Hastings as the solitary female voice opposing flogging, while scolding women who support it: "If women do not want barbarities, let them show it by public condemnation of every flogging sentence, or at least by some sort of support of those who have to undo their hysterical and disgraceful work. But, sir, we shall not expect any such thing! The ladies are sensationalists."[44] In a convoluted way, Hastings coopts authority by inventing a male persona while, at the same time, turning the anti-flogging discussion into a conversation between men: a sensible masculine correspondent discussing female sensationalism and irrationality with a male editor. In this polarized world of hysterical women and rational men, Hastings is explicitly singled out as an exception—a kind of ungendered anomaly. She surreptitiously enacts the privileged part of the token gifted female by inhabiting a multitude of subjectivities.

In an ad hoc column run in the letters section, Stafford's voice was also used to deride the supposed stupidity of women in public life, making such pronouncements as "men are their [women's] natural victims [...]. All nations at their manliest have 'kept their women down.' It is no easy task, this, but a perpetual fight against enervation!"[45] If this is parody, it is remarkably close to the views expressed in Hastings's signed writings from this period, in which she asserts that women are "nothing except by relation to men," whom they "vampirise" of their vital energy.[46] Thus Hastings began to "out-Bax Bax," sounding like a caricature of the anti-feminist that she began her career by flouting. Readers (now aware that Tina and Hastings were one-and-the-same) were confused: as one correspondent observed, "Mrs. Hastings' method of attacking the women's movement to-day is as violent and personal as her method of defending it used to be."[47] For her readers, Hastings's contradictory writings refused to coalesce into a perceptibly unified *oeuvre* or perspective.

Fabricating male personae with which to articulate her anti-woman screed was one means for Hastings to deflect charges of inconsistency. Overlapping with Edward Stafford was Sydney Robert West, invented to do battle with fellow staffers J. M. Kennedy and Alfred E. Randall—whom Hastings boasted in her memoir had never known that she had perpetrated this deception on them.[48] Writing as West, Hastings coopts a condescending masculine voice to accuse these staff writers of displaying newfound sympathy for the women's movement, which contradicts their known history of anti-feminism. The attack on Randall seems to be based on either a misunderstanding or a trumped up charge: the remark that spurred Hastings's response was made in Randall's review of a book on English patriotism, in which he writes that the author's definition of patriotism is so broad that it should extend to the "whole-souled devotion of the suffragists."[49] It is clear that Randall is being ironic—implying that even the outlandish suffragists are deserving of the label of patriot according to this author's half-baked definition of the term—but Hastings either misses the irony or pretends that she does. Writing as West in the letters section, she calls Randall out on his supposed inconsistency, demanding, "Who is ignorant of A. E. Randall's opinion of the suffragettes and of women as a class? If anyone has convinced us of the pathological origins of these indecent tussles [of suffragists] with policemen [...], he has. If anyone has suggested that the descent of the so-called educated woman into the arts has dragged all things low, that man is Mr. Randall."[50]

Kennedy draws Hastings's fire with an essay that celebrates the achievements of several university women, including the renowned classicist Jane Harrison, whom Hastings had lauded in the voice of D. Triformis. Now writing as West, Hastings charges that Kennedy's "new found chivalry" is disingenuous and that he "has as little call as Mr. Randall to be philandering with the 'monstrous regiment of women.'" The three go round for several issues before West is given the last word. Hastings takes evident pleasure in seeming to best the erudite and influential male staffer, boasting, in West's voice, "[Kennedy] has allowed me to lead him on to appear to throw over everything he cherishes most, and all for the sake of discomfiting me, an obscure nobody."[51] Clearly, Hastings could not attack Kennedy under her own name in this same way: leaving aside the question of whether or not it would be politic, the "Hastings" imprimatur simply carried too much baggage by 1913. Kennedy would be well aware of the militant feminist views espoused by Beatrice Tina, one persona now publically outed; and, as an insider, he may have known that Triformis was another of Hastings's voices. To accuse Kennedy of changing his stripes where women were concerned, Hastings— who had veered in the opposite direction, from feminism to anti-feminism—clearly needed to assume the guise of "an obscure nobody." The ever-mutable Hastings, under cover of her male alias, concludes with a sentence that underscores the clandestine irony of her own situation: "Evolution must be more gradual than this when it takes place in public."[52]

This ambivalent rhetorical act—wherein the sole female staffer of an influential English weekly usurps masculine authority to rout her male counterparts, only to outdo them in their misogyny—underscores the complexity of the ideological work performed by Hastings's pseudonyms within the spheres of feminism and anti-feminism. Tom Villis reads Hastings's drift toward anti-feminism as "a desperate and ultimately unsuccessful attempt to be accepted...[in] the male literary field in which she was writing."[53] This assumes that Hastings's remained inwardly, in some comprehensible way, feminist, or that she simply succumbed to the anti-feminism of the male writers around her. Yet the anti-feminism of Hastings's male pseudonyms is as complex as the feminism of her female personae. While expressing misogynist views under her own signature and using Stafford to ruthlessly mock women in public life, Hastings was rhetorically crossdressing to cross swords with her male colleagues, unbeknownst to them. At the same time, she was employing T.K.L to effectively lampoon a whole host of male modernists, including Wyndham Lewis, T.E. Hulme, T.S. Eliot, Richard Aldington, and, at great length, Ezra Pound: as Ann Ardis explains, "utterly unintimidated by Pound's self-positioning as the 'impresario of modernism,'" for two months in 1913, she "churned out wicked satire" at his expense.[54] Without underestimating the misogyny that Hastings expressed in her own voice and in those of her male pseudonyms, I suggest that such jousting with these self-assigned male authorities can be read as a rebellious, resourceful, and creative act—a way of negotiating male print culture that involved not only capitulation (as Villis argues), but also defiance.

West and Stafford were relatively short-lived aliases, and Hastings did not remain permanently aligned with their extreme anti-feminism. Indeed, Ann Ardis has argued that it is with her last major *New Age* persona, Alice Morning (1914-1916), that Hastings "offers her most powerful feminist 'impressions' of everyday life," while continuing to critically engage other feminists.[55] Hastings's use of multiple voices extended beyond the pages of *The New Age*, centrally defining her work as a writer.[56] Within the volatile spheres of feminist and anti-feminist debate, pseudonyms allowed Hastings to experiment in voice and perspective; to change argumentative tack; and, finally to refuse *all* settled positions.

NOTES

1. Margaret Beetham, "Periodicals and the New Media: Women and Imagined Communities." *Women's Studies International Forum* 29 (2006): 231-240; 238.

2. Ibid, 239.

3. Philip Mairet, *A. R. Orage: A Memoir* (London: Dent and Sons, 1936), 47.

4. Hastings lists Beatrice Tina, T.K.L., Alice Morning, D. Triformis, Edward Stafford, and Sydney Robert West, along with the "passing pseudonyms" "V.M., G. Whiz, J. Wilson, T.W., A.M.A., Cynius, etc." (*The Old "New Age": Orage and Others.* London: New Age Press, 1936, 43. Hereafter ONAO). The Modernist Journals Project (MJP) website adds 7 more to this list.

5. Stephen Gray, *Beatrice Hastings: A Literary Life.* (Johannesburg, South Africa: Viking [Penguin], 2004), 234.

6. T.K.L., "Pastiche," *The Straight-Thinker*, January 23, 1932, 8.

7. In his memoir, Mairet inadvertently switches between "Tina" and "Hastings" and indexes the author's name as "Tina," suggesting that this early persona eclipsed Hastings's myriad later ones (ibid, 71).

8. For comparison, Tina has 30 items (including articles, letters, and a serialized novella) and one book attributed to her name; Triformis has 17; Edward Stafford, 9; and Sydney Robert West, 4.

9. Two informative studies that comment on Hastings's shift to anti-feminism are Lucy Delap, "Feminist and anti-feminist encounters in Edwardian Britain." *Historical Research* 78, no. 201 (August 2005): 377-399; and Tom Villis, *Reaction and the Avant-Garde: The Revolt Against Liberal Democracy in Early Twentieth-Century Britain* (London: Tauris Academic Studies, 2006), 174-191. However, neither Delap nor Villis examine Hastings's male pseudonyms, nor do they dwell on the rhetorical affordances of Hastings's pseudonyms per se.

10. Delap, "Feminist and Anti-Feminist," 396. See also Villis, 174-191.

11. Sean Latham maintains that *The New Age* "began its life as a passionate advocate of women's rights" in his "Introduction to Volume I" on the Modernist Journals Project website. In "Debating Feminism, Modernism, and Socialism: Beatrice Hastings's Voices in *The New Age*," Ann Ardis stresses that *The New Age* was unusual among socialist papers in devoting so much space to the women's movement (Bonnie Kime Scott, ed., *Gender in Modernism: New Geographies, Complex Intersections* [Urbana and Chicago, University of Illinois Press, 1907], 160-171: 161.) Hereafter "Debating Feminism." On feminism in *The New Age*, see also Lee Garver, "The Political Katherine Mansfield." *Modernism/modernity* 8, no. 2 (April 2001): 225-243.

12. Villis, ibid, 174.

13. "Notes of the Week," *The New Age*, August 22 1912, 388.

14. Marsden, "The Woman Movement and the 'Ablest Socialists,'" *Freewoman* 2:41 (August 19, 1912): 281-285; 281.

15. Hastings writes, "I took enormous pains not to be identified" (ONAO 8). Bennett also avoided detection, for he was asked to review his own fiction under his pseudonym "Tonson;" in contrast, Hastings writes that Kennedy "was known to be 'S. Verdad' by many persons. There was no deep mystery about his contributions" (ONAO 22).

16. Gray, ibid, 160.

17. Hastings, ONAO, 8.

18. Ibid.

19. Bax, "Feminism and Female Suffrage," *The New Age*, May 30 1908, 88.

20. Tina (Beatrice Hastings), "Woman as State Creditor" *The New Age*, June 27, 1908, 169.

21. Ibid.

22. Mark Gaipa, "E. (Edith) Nesbit 1858-1924," Modernist Journals Project website.

23. *The New Age*, July 4, 1908, 197-8.

24. A Reluctant Suffragette (Beatrice Hastings), "The Other Women," *The New Age*, July 4, 1908, 187.

25. Tina (Beatrice Hastings), "The Case of the Anti-Feminists," *The New Age*, August 29, 1908, 349.

26. Delap, "Feminist and Anti-Feminist," 395.

27. Ibid.

28. Beatrice (Tina) Hastings, Correspondence, *The New Age*, May 19, 1910, 69.

29. See John Mullan, *Anonymity: A Secret History of English Literature* (London: Faber and Faber, 2007) and Robert J. Griffin, *The Faces of Anonymity: Anonymous and Pseudonymous Publications from the Sixteenth to the Twentieth Century* (NY: Palgrave, 2003).

30. Gray states that the author adopted the name "Hastings" by 1906 (Gray, ibid, 142), but Fabian Society records (held at the London School of Economics) confirm that she held a membership from June 1907 to June 1909 as Beatrice Tina. She advertised a room to let as Beatrice Tina in the November 4, 1909 issue of *The New Age*, 23.

31. F.G. Howe, Letter to the Editor, *The New Age*, February 17, 1910, 381.

32. Triformis (Beatrice Hastings), "Militancy and Humanity," *The New Age*, January 6, 1910, 225; and "The Failure of Militancy," *The New Age*, January 20, 1910, 273.

33. As Ann Ardis notes, we lack the archival evidence that could clarify her attitude ("Debating Feminism," 163).

34. Advertisements regularly appear throughout 1909 and 1910 for *Woman's Worst Enemy: Woman*. It is praised effusively as "Book of the Week" in the July 22, 1909 issue of the *The New Age* (254), and a notice in the November 17, 1910 Literary Supplement calls the failure to include the book in the Fabian "What to Read" pamphlet an "egregious omission" (*The New Age*, 8).

35. Triformis (Beatrice Hastings), "A Fallacy Behind the Militant Theory," *The New Age*, February 3, 1910, 323.

36. Correspondence, *The New Age*, February 17, 1910, 380.

37. Triformis (Beatrice Hastings), "Why Not," *The New Age*, March 17, 1910, 462.

38. Ibid.

39. Correspondence, *The New Age*, April 14, 1910, 573.

40. Triformis (Beatrice Hastings), "Women and Freedom," *The New Age*, May 12, 1910, 30.

41. Correspondence, Beatrice (Tina) Hastings, *The New Age*, May 19, 1910, 69.

42. For instance, Pagan (in "A Modern Bacchante," *The New Age*, August 29, 1907, 279); Triformis, in such pieces as "Women and Freedom" (ibid); and A Reluctant Suffragette. Lucy Delap elaborates on an important individualist strand of Edwardian feminism in her book, *The Feminist Avant-Garde: Transatlantic Encounters of the Early Twentieth Century* (Cambridge University Press, 2007), 102-138.

43. Delap, "Feminist and Anti-Feminist Encounters," 397. Hastings writes in the April 17, 1913 issue that she has "small reason to respect women individually or as a sex; but much to despise them," referencing the "white slave agitation" as "proof" of women's "unrestrained mania for brutal and dangerous purification by punishment" (*The New Age*, 592). On the White Slave Traffic Bill (or Criminal Law Amendment Act of 1912), see Angus McLaren, *The Trials of Masculinity: Policing Sexual Boundaries, 1870-1930* (Cambridge University Press, 2003), 18.

44. Edward Stafford (Beatrice Hastings), Correspondence ("The White Slave Act"), *The New Age*, February 20, 1913, 390.

45. Edward Stafford, "Women in Public," *The New Age*, October 9, 1913, 709.

46. Beatrice Hastings, Correspondence, *The New Age*, May 8, 1913, 46 and August 7, 1913, 439.

47. George Hirst, Correspondence, *The New Age*, April 17, 1913, 591.

48. Hastings, ONAO, 43.

49. A.E.R., "Views and Reviews," *The New Age*, May 1, 1913, 15.

50. S. West, "Feminism in the 'New Age,'" *The New Age*, May 8, 1913, 47.

51. S. West, "Feminism," *The New Age*, June 19, 1913, 214.

52. Ibid.

53. Villis, ibid, 190.

54. Ardis, "The Dialogics of Modernism(s) in the New Age," *Modernism/ modernity*, 14:3 (2007): 421.

55. Ardis, "Debating Feminism," 165. As Alice Morning, she wrote a regular column 1914-1916; three pieces in 1918; and one piece in 1920.

56. Along with T.K.L., Hastings revived Alice Morning in *The Straight-Thinker* in 1932. She also published several of her own long works anonymously in that publication, including *A Psychic's Diary*, a semi-autobiographical piece that records the experience of channeling different spirit voices, suggesting that Hastings's multi-vocal writing was expressive of a deep psychological tendency.

BEATRICE HASTINGS AND THE WAR ON MATERNITY

Erin M. Kingsley

ERIN KINGSLEY is an assistant professor at King University in Tennessee. She received a Ph.D. from the University of Colorado in 2014, and her articles on modernism and post-modernism can be found in Critique: Studies in Contemporary Fiction, Philological Quarterly, *and* Virginia Woolf Miscellany.

In "Woman as State Creditor" (June 27, 1908), one of the most notable diatribes in *The New Age*, Beatrice Hastings creates a horrific picture of childbirth in Britain at the turn of the twentieth century. Writing as "Beatrice Tina" (one of Hastings's many pen names and the pseudonym she often employed to discuss maternity), Hastings attacks virtually every socio-cultural construction of the female physical reproductive process, a multiple and diffuse experience which she often terms simply "maternity." Hastings, an under-read modernist writer and a "self-claimed shadow coeditor" of *The New Age* from 1907-1914, claims in "State Creditor" that women "conspire to lie about maternity."[1] She explains, "The torture of child-birth is the ugliest fact of human life. Women instinctively veil its horrors from that sensitive creature, the husband."[2]

Hastings's argument surrounding the "horrors" of parturition hinges on the claim that the "ignorant" birthing woman is marooned as she attempts to weather the storm of childbirth guided only by her similarly "ignorant" husband who is figured as a "creature" (one of her favorite words): something ill-formed and not quite human. In her view, laboring women receive no assistance from men or from scientific and medical advancements; instead, women remain subjected to extreme pain and even death. And because women either have no alternative (the option of "self governance" being unavailable to them) or because they are unnaturally attached to their husbands, they conspire to lie. In Hastings's view, women cover the horrific experience of parturition with glowing falsehoods about the honor of motherhood to ensure that future generations of unassuming, naïve, and dim-witted women will sign up for the same experience of reproduction and thus unquestioningly further the tide of humanity.

Hastings further attests in "State Creditor" that once a woman is allowed to self govern by winning the vote and other legal benefits, she will necessarily choose freedom and eschew the constricting state of maternal slavery, which Hastings deems a "disability."[3] Anticipating Virginia Woolf, whose *A Room of One's Own* (1929) betrays tremendous anxiety over female birth, Hastings similarly connects the enfleshed experience of pregnancy and childbirth to a loss of freedom, asserting that "women love liberty of mind and body as much as" men do.[4] Yet, this liberty is forcibly taken from women as they are subjected to the "ordeal" of childbirth "year after year, in health and out of health, just as long as the poor thing can endure it and live."[5] In Hastings's barbed one-page article, the incredibly complex and historically-engrained battle of the sexes is mapped in miniature. But why, the reader may ask, was Hastings so angry about maternity, a seemingly "natural" aspect of a normative woman's life?

The answer to Hastings's anger is more complex than it appears to be at first glance. Hastings harbored valid complaints against a socio-economic system that used and abused women and their bodies, but I also claim that Hastings was more than just a political writer. Instead, she purposely cultivated an aesthetics of unease, nurturing her acerbic writerly persona to agitate her reading public, thereby furthering timely conversations about the role of women in the rapidly-shifting culture of the modernist era. Just as her pen names continually shift, so too do Hastings's readers experience persistent destabilization in the face of her relentless linguistic attacks. Hastings sought to "shame and subdue" her detractors "by exhibiting mental force."[6]

An additional aspect of Hastings's anger stems from the construction of "maternity" itself, which is nuanced and complex. Defined by the *Oxford English Dictionary* as both the state of being pregnant *and* of being a mother, and the qualities that "motherliness" should possess, any conception of maternity that Hastings held was indelibly linked to the politics of women, work, and the vote in the early twentieth century.[7] While this chapter does not delve into Hastings's many other arguments surrounding "the woman question," including the issue of suffrage and of suffragettes, the role of the Women's Social and Political Union (W.S.P.U.), and the relationship between women and labor, she wrote extensively about these concerns throughout her hundreds of publications in *The New Age* and in her slim book, *Woman's Worst Enemy: Woman.*[8] What is more, Hastings harbored a virulent distaste for women's suffrage, believing that feminists like Emmeline and Christabel Pankhurst single-mindedly pursued the vote as a panacea to cure the ills of a panoply of socio-economic injustices towards women. "I never urge the vote," Hastings explains, "as a means primarily of getting anything but the recognition that as women we are national citizens."[9] Hastings was additionally frustrated by the mistreatment of prisoners, a thorny social problem that feminist organizations like the W.S.P.U. refused to address as they focused on the vote for women alone. "But still," Hastings writes, "it can all wait until we get the vote! Pah! One gets to hate the very word 'vote.'"[10]

Hastings was known as an attack dog of sorts, "bursting with journalistic fervour"; her taste for fame was reportedly unrivaled, and she tore into her critics and her self-authored articles alike with verve and vitriol—she would often pen an article under one name, then assail this same article with a different point of view using an alternate pseudonym.[11] This self-reflexive, polyvocal hybridity is at the root of what makes Beatrice Hastings so dizzyingly unique in the modernist period and so maddeningly ephemeral. Even her sole biographer, Stephen Gray, concludes with puzzlement, "Until the very end we will not know if she was fiercely capable or a crackpot, her hardscrabble life a triumph or a defeat."[12] Impossible to pin down due to her rapid-fire changes in stance and her arsenal of pseudonyms, Hastings explained that she remained virtually anonymous so that she could continue to keep *The New Age* afloat: "I cared for nothing but the paper, that was my life. I am far from regretting it, either, for the work will eventually come back to my door, and I could not have done it if exposed to the publicity I should have had by signing every thing..."[13]

Hastings's writerly persona(s), her aesthetics of unease, and the various causes she championed are crucial aspects undergirding the significance of Hastings's multi-pronged attack on maternity and motherhood in her book, articles, and letters to the editor published in *The New Age*. But because Hastings was firmly rooted in the political, social, and economic reality of early twentieth-century England, it is useful to examine the social context of maternity in her time period before we consider Hastings's acerbic portrayal of maternity itself.

To begin, it is important to understand the then-contemporary notion of eugenic reproduction and its ties to larger hegemonic issues of state and country. A letter-writer in *The New Age* addresses eugenics succinctly by claiming "[o]ne of the first principles of Eugenics is that a mother should prepare herself for maternity."[14]

The predominant cultural narrative of the early twentieth century was that it was woman's responsibility to reproduce, thereby reproducing British empire and even the Anglo-Saxon "race" itself.[15] The empire had recently experienced its first direct challenges to its power, from the Boer agitation in 1899-1902 to the Irish Home Rule movement, the rising women's suffrage movement and "cyclical economic recessions, organized labour unrest," and "socialist revival."[16] Due to the high number of recruits deemed unacceptable for service in the Boer War because of "physical inadequacy," a vast cultural movement began in Britain to reeducate and train able-bodied men and women, especially mothers and pregnant women via the mothercraft movement.[17] Not only did Britain need more bodies, it needed good ones—and breeding better stock lies at the heart of eugenicist discourse.[18]

The mothercraft movement was concerned with the proper education of British mothers and was rooted in a widespread cultural belief that if one could influence the mothers, one could influence future generations and change an entire empire—even the entire globe.[19] The push for mothercraft was also intimately connected to the women's movement and the new cultural emphasis on Darwinism. Some women even claimed that if the larger female population was adequately equipped to teach their own children, this education would necessarily affect the choice of future husbands and improve the morality of those husbands: "Sexual selection would again come to the fore [...] with the female playing the leading role as her ancestors had done."[20] To these ends, organizations were formed to canvas lower-class neighborhoods and hold meetings to instruct mothers in areas as diverse as diet, lifestyle, care of infants and children, and proper management of the household. Jane Lewis argues this intrusive movement helped to displace ingrained maternal systems of care (traditional advice passed down from mother to daughter) by pushing a very specifically middle-class, uniform agenda on whole communities.[21] Indeed, the mothercraft movement was another method by which hegemonic British culture attempted to control the power inherent in reproduction, and to harness such reproduction to the needs and ends of the greater British empire.

These tremendous and rapid social changes in tandem with the heightened response to maternity created an entirely new cultural interest in pregnancy and reproduction that began to flourish in Britain in the early twentieth century. The appearance of the pregnant female body in public space as mass-produced maternity clothes became available around 1910 is an additional contributor towards the cultural attention paid to maternity. This burgeoning scrutiny, in turn, was both fueled by and elicited numerous responses from writers grappling with the meaning and representation of pregnancy in light of the heightened nationalized interest in reproduction. Because pregnancy and childbirth were integral to new conversations about the relations between the sexes and were central to both the rise of first-wave feminism and the plunging birth rates, a heightened concern over reproduction began to manifest itself specifically in the British media, appearing in publications authored by men and women alike. These publications ranged from monographs exploring scientific reproduction to "self-help" handbooks directing a pregnant woman's behaviors, but, importantly, many appeared in the cheap and quick print media of newspapers, journals, and circulars. Thus, a new conversation about the "now" of reproduction was created—a conversation happening in real time about real-time issues.[22]

An additional aspect of Hastings's argument against maternity is the socio-economic toll reproduction takes on women. Hastings was rightfully dismayed over the cultural push for women to birth more babies and to birth them well without providing them the proper apparatus to survive and thrive while nourishing these new lives. For example, Hastings argues in her slim book, *Woman's Worst Enemy: Woman* (published by *The New Age* and heavily advertised therein) that for all of England's big budget, "not one farthing is voted for the aid of mothers," and that their thankless and unpaid labor for the good of the state is the cheapest labor of all.[23] Hastings consistently pursues her notion of human rights in her writing, especially the rights of underprivileged members of society like women, lower-class workers, and prisoners. Her conception of maternity is heavily informed by her ontology of state-ordered and state-paid labor, a system that in her view should be balanced by consent from both parties (the state and the worker), full and complete information about the nature of the labor and of the contract, and proper reimbursement. For Hastings, the pregnant and birthing woman is a tool of the state; thus, she should naturally have access to the rights and wages of any other state worker. Hastings's anger stems from the fact that women are so slighted by the state: so necessary to its colonial and war time endeavors, yet so ill provided for.

Hastings was not the only voice calling for state support of pregnancy, childbirth, and the post-natal period. Organizations like the Women's Cooperative Guild, which published an important collection of working women's testimonies about the hardships of pregnancy and childbirth entitled *Maternity: Letters From Working Women* in 1915, pushed for state support in the early years of the century. Partially due to their efforts, small changes in legislation began to appear. The National Insurance Act of 1911 provided maternity benefits including a 30 shilling bonus paid directly to the mother, while the Factory Act of 1891 ensured that if she was a worker, she would not return to work until at least one month after giving birth.[24] Unfortunately, this one-month period was without pay, which was why the paid maternity benefits recommended by the Women's Cooperative Guild were so crucial. The Midwives' Act of 1902 guaranteed that the midwife who attended the average woman had received at least a modicum of training. And the Maternity and Child Welfare Act in 1918 established committees to monitor health, properly pay midwives, cover health visits, and provide "infant-welfare centres, day nurseries, and food supplements" for the needy.[25]

Many of these small steps in supporting gestating women occurred years after Hastings's articles in *The New Age*, articles which go beyond merely critiquing the social apparatus surrounding physical reproduction.[26] In *Woman's Worst Enemy: Woman*, Hastings denigrates the entire reproductive process— marriage, sex, pregnancy, gestation, parturition, and maternal nurturing. Tracing the curse of childbirth back to Adam and Eve in the Genesis chapter of the Bible, Hastings claims "the womb is fashioned for torment, but it is fashioned also to crave its own torment."[27] The concept of women perpetuating one of the single greatest ills in their lives, that of maternity, loops back to the title of Hastings's book and explains why indeed women are their own worst enemies. Birthing women are harmed not only by the cultural and patriarchal indifference to the particular demands of maternity, then—women themselves invite this torture. Because Hastings argues elsewhere that "women are born, not made," she clearly believes that despite the molding of culture, there is something in the bloodstream of women to continue to make them "women."[28] She thus pinpoints the primary battle in the larger war against the ills of maternity to be not that of women versus men, but women versus nature.[29] Achieving the vote will not help women's situation in Hastings's view, for they will remain women: weak at heart, seduced by the call of maternity, beholden to their bodies in ways masculine bodies will never be.

Hastings's word choice is also noteworthy: "the womb is fashioned for torment, but it is fashioned also to crave its own torment."[30] The *OED* defines "fashioned" as a term usually employed to describe a non-human artifact (for example, stockings) that is made with great skill.[31] In Hastings's construction, she likens a female body part—perhaps *the* female body part, as the womb or vagina is often synecdochal for woman herself—to a flimsy, decorative yet artfully-designed piece of woman's clothing that is cheap to purchase and essentially disposable. Her next noteworthy word, "torment," is indicative of both the spiritual suffering of hell (where one is sent when one deserves it) and the man-made torture chamber.[32] The word "torment" is doubly interesting here, because an individual can be subjected to torment, and he or she can also *become* a torment.[33] Her use of the word "torment" therefore supports her characterization of the womb as both an element of torture (functioning as the tortured subject) and desirous of this same torture (functioning as the torturer). Finally, "crave" is yet another demeaning term, meaning "to demand," "to beg, especially as a gift or favour," and to have an appetite for.[34] Hastings thus gestures towards the traditional meaning of "hysteria" (a word often applied to suffragettes at the time) as the condition of having a wandering womb that, based on its appetites or cravings, could manifest itself at any location in a woman's body at any given time.[35] The womb and the desire for reproduction that Hastings's representative woman displays here is palimpsestically laden with connotations of a cheap and fashionable act, the torturous condition of a tormentor, the ministrations of a demanding and troublesome individual, and the hysterical appetites of an unruly suffragette.

Returning to Hastings's most developed piece about maternity, "Woman as State Creditor" (which she apparently deemed so important that it appears both in *The New Age* and in *Woman's Worst Enemy*), it is important to note that Hastings categorizes maternity as chiefly a "disability," an event that simultaneously causes harm and, in a more perfect world, would provoke the state to provide more funds to pay for this harm. Hastings attacks the state for providing no "legislation on the matter"—nothing to ensure, for example, that the pregnant woman would not continue bearing children until her eventual death from exhaustion.[36] Hastings claims that a "woman's parliament" would rescue such women from multiply experiencing "agonies no man would face once, let alone twice."[37] Any argument Hastings constructs about maternity is therefore indelibly linked to larger arguments about the treatment of women in the patriarchal nation-state, and the foolish attempts to keep women from gaining multiple rights like the right to work, the right to vote, the right to divorce—in short, any right that men held.[38]

"Woman as State Creditor" received an impressive number of printed responses in *The New Age*. The issue printed immediately after "State Creditor" includes no less than five letters reacting to Hastings's diatribe. One response states that "[m]ost women are not such cowards and prudes" when it comes to being fearful of childbirth, while another letter-writer thanks Hastings for "rendering articulate the cry" of women who similarly "think the price of a child too dear…"[39] Hastings, continuing to write under the name "Tina," counters the letters her article has garnered in the July 11, 1908 issue of *The New Age*, and "State Creditor" continues to resonate with future article-writers, who mention her piece as alternately "ingenious" and as sorely in need of a "corrective."[40]

Beyond Hastings's reasonable if not acerbic arguments that the system surrounding women's reproductive health and rights was broken, even non-existent, her anger remains. At root, she harbors extreme rage that is impossible to distinguish from her afore-mentioned aesthetics of unease. Was this rage due to personal experience? Stephen Gray calls it a "truth" that "by the end of 1897, a child of hers had died," but this element of Hastings's biography lies in shadow.[41] It is also questionable whether any discussion of Hastings's linguistic war on maternity should even mention her own possible motherhood, although she most certainly experienced parturition at one point or another. Early in *Woman's Worst Enemy*, she writes, "I bear the stigma on my soul of an unwilling maternity," explaining that going through childbirth was a "rude shock of knowledge" which "showed me a yawning pit of human pain; and this abyss, I was told, was the way all women had to go."[42] Again, Hastings employs language directly linked to hell and to despair; her chosen rhetoric surrounding the birthing experience would be at home in Dante's *Inferno*. Importantly, Hastings links her hatred of birthgiving to a natural facet of her being: "Never, at any time of my whole existence, did I want to become a mother," she claims.[43] Just as the machinery of Britain asserts that women are born to be mothers, Hastings counters with her own equal and opposite contention that women are also born not to be mothers.

Women as women, not mothers, was an inflammatory idea in Hastings's age. In a 1911 letter in *Everybody's Magazine*, the author, W.B.E., attests that women must realize two important facts: they exist solely to reproduce, and they alone are responsible for the "moral character" of their children, and thus the entire British race.[44] Such letters attempting to remind the modern working woman of her bodily duty to reproduce as birth rates plunged alarmingly are quite common in the early years of the century, and illustrate the great extent to which the new public conception of pregnancy and childbirth went paired with eugenic sentiments and with the first wave of feminism. As women like Hastings began to jettison traditional routes like marriage and family and entered the workforce, the fear that the birth rate would continue to plunge and the national "stock" would continue to suffer skyrocketed.

Hastings perfectly encapsulates the specific historical moment of the transition between woman as solely wife and mother and woman as career-driven individual, and the tensions and fears this shift engendered. Beyond her personal feelings about maternity, her hyperbolic writing style when discussing gestation and parturition and its effect on a woman's life was purposely acerbic to generate conversation around a topic she viewed as vital to human rights and to the women's movement. When she writes in *Woman's Worst Enemy*, "Never have I seen the adult creature of whom I would like to be the mother," it is because for Hastings, everything about the "unwilling" transition to motherhood smacks of a loss of what she terms "royal freedom."[45] The sovereignty over her own corporeal experience, Hastings claims, is directly linked to a power and authority so exalted and vital that it is best termed "royal." It is an official possession each woman should grasp as a fundamentally human right that they are born with. It is a right that each woman should have the opportunity to *choose*, with equal power and authority, to relinquish. For Hastings, the "unwilling" aspect of maternity is the most pernicious.

And yet at root there is still Hastings's distaste for the "adult creature" and for the role of motherhood. With the use of a word like "creature," she once again distances herself from the humanity of maternity, likening the process to an inhuman and unnaturally hellish experience that just does not coalesce with the normative— even the *sane*—woman's life. She admits that some women find a "sensuous and spiritual enjoyment" in becoming a "perfect mother," a mother who "suffers nothing in delivering a child."[46] That Hastings would include so many references to the specious and harming cultural construction of the totemic "woman as perfect mother" figure is alarming and somewhat jarring. In the midst of her well-founded criticism of maternity, there lies a portrait of motherhood so glossy and perfect that it is not surprising Hastings is enraged when she cannot live up to such high expectations— expectations she partially manufactures and facilitates. There is no easy accounting for the juxtaposition of these two figures of the mother in Hastings, and this disjunction only increases her status as a writer who functions primarily in the aesthetics of unease.

Hastings was a shimmering chimera, a cipher of early twentieth-century women's issues appearing palimpsestically in each one of her writerly personas. In her telling series of articles in *The New Age* and in her book *Woman's Worst Enemy*, the reader can begin to understand that maternity for Hastings was the lynchpin in the larger issue of women's rights. For Hastings, maternity was a *human* rights issue that transcended the significance of merely achieving the vote, and instead represented the dark and labyrinthine heart of the human experience.

NOTES

1. Ann Ardis, "Introduction to Debating Feminism, Modernism, and Socialism: Beatrice Hastings's Voices in *The New Age*," in *Gender in Modernism: New Geographies, Complex Intersections*, ed. Bonnie Kime Scott (Urbana and Chicago: University of Illinois Press, 2007): 161; Beatrice Tina (Hastings), "Woman as State Creditor," *The New Age*, June 27, 1908, 169. While Hastings's given name at birth was Emily Alice Haigh, Hastings regularly employed at least 13 pseudonyms: "Tina, Robert á Field, T.K.L., Alice Morning, D. Triformis, Edward Stafford, S. Robert West, V.M., G. Whiz, J. Wilson, T.W., A.M.A., and Cynicus." Ardis, "Introduction to Debating Feminism," 161. Robert Scholes records additional pen names for Hastings, including Pagan, E.H., B.L.H., Annette Doorly, Hastings Lloyd, and Mrs. Malaprop. Robert Scholes, "Hastings, Beatrice (Emily Alice Haigh) (1879-1943)," The Modernist Journals Project, accessed April 14, 2015, www.modjourn.org.

2. Tina (Beatrice Hastings), "Woman as State Creditor," 169.

3. Ibid.

4. Ibid.

5. Ibid.

6. Beatrice Tina (Beatrice Hastings), "The Case of the Anti-Feminists," *The New Age*, August 29, 1908, 349.

7. "maternity, n.," *OED Online*, March 2015, Oxford University Press, accessed April 20, 2015, www.oed.com.

8. Sean Latham, "The Mess and Muddle of Modernism: The Modernist Journals Project and Modern Periodical Studies," *Tulsa Studies in Women's Literature* 30.2 (Fall 2011): 409. Note that while Latham cites Hastings as having penned approximately 113 articles in *The New Age*, if one considers the numerous known and unknown pseudonyms that Hastings employed, she actually published much more. My thanks to Ben Johnson for pointing this out.

9. D. Triformis (Beatrice Hastings), "Woman's Suffrage. To the Editor of 'The New Age,'" *The New Age*, April 21, 1910, 596.

10. Beatrice Hastings, "A Holiday in Gaol," *The New Age*, June 15, 1911, 165. Hastings elsewhere attacks the women's marches with this comment: "Women who imagine that by herding themselves in large numbers and parading the streets, they are proving their right to freedom, are actually proving that they are a herd with that subconscious distrust of reason which has always distinguished herds and mobs." D. Triformis (Beatrice Hastings), "Women and Freedom," *The New Age*, May 12, 1910, 29.

11. John Carswell, *Lives and Letters: A.R. Orage, Beatrice Hastings,*

Katherine Mansfield, John Middleton Murry, S.S. Koteliansky, 1906–1957 (New York: New Directions, 1978), 33. Note that Stephen Gray, Hastings's only extant biographer, claims that Carswell is among the "semi-reliables: when [Carswell] had no documentary proof of a salacious detail of Beatrice's life, at least he had the tact to leave it out." Stephen Gray, *Beatrice Hastings: A Literary Life* (London: Viking, 2004), 6. For an example of Hastings arguing against herself while employing different pseudonyms, see D. Triformis (a pseudonym of Hastings), "Women and Freedom," in which Triformis takes "Miss Beatrice Hastings" to task for writing "one of the most foolish fancies of the average thoughtless woman." Triformis, "Women and Freedom," 30.

12. Gray, *Beatrice Hastings*, 11.

13. Beatrice Hastings, *The Old "New Age": Orange and Others*, in *Gender in Modernism: New Geographies, Complex Intersections*, edited by Bonnie Kime Scott (Urbana and Chicago: University of Illinois Press, 2007), 176.

14. Eugenist, "Mrs. Braby's 'Downward,' To the Editor of 'The New Age,'" *The New Age*, April 28, 1910, 620.

15. As Lucy Bland explains, the term "race" was often employed at the turn of the century, especially by feminists, and it carried intentional "slippage between human race, white race, and Anglo-Saxon race, and the assumption of white superiority and supremacy." I therefore use "race" in much the same way, as an indicator of the hegemonic manifestations of a specific racial and cultural group. Lucy Bland, *Banishing the Beast: Sexuality and the Early Feminists* (New York: The New York Press, 1995), 70.

16. Ibid., 223.

17. Ibid., 83.

18. For Hastings's most notable comments on eugenics, see Beatrice Tina (Hastings), *Woman's Worst Enemy: Woman* (London: The New Age Press, 1909). Hastings claims therein that "men's cruel suppression" of scientists and their advances keep women getting pregnant with unwanted children, "to whom they bequeath a failing generative energy, which finally weakens the whole nation into sterility and ignominious decay" (6). See especially the chapters entitled "The Two Curses" and "The Plight of the Unfit Mother."

19. For more information on mothercraft, see Jane Lewis, *The Politics of Motherhood: Child and Maternal Welfare in England, 1900–1939* (Montreal: McGill-Queen's University Press, 1980).

20. Bland, *Banishing the Beast*, 84.

21. Lewis, *The Politics of Motherhood*, 20.

22. The real-time conversation about reproduction at the turn of the century cannot be separated from the larger conversation about women's rights and the women's suffrage movement. Lisa Tickner explains that the suffrage movement, much like the rise of the cultural conversation surrounding maternity

that Hastings was a vital aspect of, was "the first to exploit new publicity methods made possible by the rise of national, daily, penny and halfpenny newspapers...." Lisa Tickner, *The Spectacle of Women: Imagery of the Suffrage Campaign 1907-14* (Chicago: The University of Chicago Press, 1988), xii. While I do not have the space to cover the women's movement here, I am aware that any conversation Hastings held surrounding maternity and women's bodies is a critical aspect of this larger conversation about women's rights. See Tickner for an excellent gloss of the historical arch of the women's movement and for reprints of the contemporary artwork surrounding the movement.

23. Tina (Beatrice Hastings), *Woman's Worst Enemy: Woman*, 23, 48. In linking the curse of maternity to Adam and Eve, Hastings anticipates another under-read female modernist writer, Olive Moore, who similarly attacks mothering and the family in her 1935 collection of aphorisms, *The Apple is Bitten Again*. Moore writes therein, "Woman is the vacuum which Nature abhors and must see filled. Consequently woman is always slightly ridiculous unless stretched on a bed or with a child in her arms. All the rest is marking time." Olive Moore, *The Apple is Bitten Again, Collected Writings* (Elmwood Park: Dalkey Archive Press, 1992), 343.

24. Clare Hanson, *A Cultural History of Pregnancy: Pregnancy, Medicine and Culture, 1750-2000* (New York: Palgrave Macmillan, 2004), 99; Barbara Brookes, "Women and Reproduction, 1860-1939," in *Labour and Love: Women's Experience of Home and Family, 1850-1940*, ed. Jane Lewis (Oxford: Basil Blackwell, 1986), 154.

25. Brookes, "Women and Reproduction, 1860-1939," 157.

26. John Carswell notes that Hastings's last article in *The New Age* appears in March 1920. She then started the small magazine *The Straight-Thinker*, penning most of the content herself. Carswell, *Lives and Letters*, 223.

27. Tina (Beatrice Hastings), *Woman's Worst Enemy: Woman*, 9.

28. Beatrice Hastings, "The Awakening of Women," *The New Age*, November 27, 1913, 125. For more on the classic argument of nature versus culture in the perpetuation of mothering, see Nancy Chodorow, who claims that mothering is not rooted in the body but is instead perpetuated by the "sex-gender system" and by mothers themselves. Nancy Chodorow, *The Reproduction of Mothering: Psychoanalysis and the Sociology of Gender* (Berkeley: University of California Press, 1978), 38, 208. Also see Julia Kristeva, who claims that the desire to mother is rooted in the female body and to resist it is to resist femininity itself. Julia Kristeva, "Women's Time," in *The Portable Kristeva*, ed. Kelly Oliver (New York: Columbia University Press, 1997), 365, 376.

29. Tina (Beatrice Hastings), *Women's Worst Enemy: Woman*, 8.

30. Ibid., 9.

31. "fashioned, adj.," *OED Online*, March 2015, Oxford University Press, www.oed.com.

32. "torment, n.," *OED Online*, March 2015, Oxford University Press, www.oed.com.

33. Ibid.

34. "crave, v.," *OED Online*, March 2015, Oxford University Press, www. oed.com.

35. For more on women as hysterical, see Sandra Gilbert and Susan Gubar, *The Madwoman in the Attic: The Woman Writer and the Nineteenth-Century Literary Imagination* (New Haven: Yale University Press, 1979). For more on the reproducing female as hysteric, see Rebecca Kukla, *Mass Hysteria: Medicine, Culture, and Mothers' Bodies* (Lanham, MD: Rowman & Littlefield, 2005). For more on suffragettes as hysterical, see chapter four, "Representation," in Tickner, *The Spectacle of Women*, especially the section titled "The Hysterical Woman and the Shrieking Sisterhood" therein.

36. Tina (Beatrice Hastings), "Woman as State Creditor," 169.

37. Ibid.

38. For more on women's rights and the lack thereof in early twentieth century Britain, see Jane Garrity, *Step-Daughters of England: British Women Modernists and the National Imaginary* (Manchester: Manchester University Press, 2003).

39. Anonymous, "Beatrice Tina and the Almighty," *The New Age*, July 4, 1908, 197; D.C.A.M., "To the Editor of The New Age," July 4, 1908, 198.

40. C.H. Norman, "The Injustice of 'Votes for Women,'" *The New Age*, July 18, 1908, 228; M.D. Eder, "Good Breeding or Eugenics," *The New Age*, July 18, 1908, 227.

41. Gray, *Beatrice Hastings*, 105.

42. Hastings, *Woman's Worst Enemy*, 3, 1.

43. Ibid., 1.

44. W.B.E., "Letter," "Once More—Woman's Sphere!" *Everybody's Magazine*, March 1911, 423.

45. Hastings, *Woman's Worst Enemy*, 9, 3, 1.

46. Ibid., 9.

"THE ENGLISH TALENT FOR ADOPTING": IMITATION, TRANSLATION, AND PARODY IN BEATRICE HASTINGS'S NEW AGE ESSAYS

Sunny Stalter-Pace

SUNNY STALTER-PACE is an associate professor at Auburn University. She is the author of Underground Movements: Modern Culture on the New York City Subway *(University of Massachusetts, 2013), and her articles on twentieth-century literature and culture have appeared in journals including* American Quarterly, Journal of Modern Literature, *and* Journal of American Drama and Theatre.

FROM September to mid-October in 1913, Ezra Pound and Beatrice Hastings had a knock-down, drag-out fight about poetry. They argued about how it should look, how it should sound, and what it should discuss. They argued about how—and even if—it should be translated. And they fought about how to fight about it. Pound repeatedly claimed that he was showing his readers the new French poetry, but that if they couldn't hear its music or appreciate its point of view it was of no concern to him. Hastings took pains to translate the chunks of verse Pound dropped into his arguments; she wrote parodies of the poems he celebrated, and she imagined increasingly more ridiculous schools to which their authors belonged. While Pound champions novelty, and particularly technical innovation, he admits of Hastings the backhanded compliment that she possesses "the English talent for adopting."[1] In this essay, I show how Hastings does her adopting through parody, using her skills as an imitator and translator in order to undercut Pound's pretension. Hastings utilizes one of the key strategies that Leonard Diepeveen locates in parodies of modernism, and indeed in parody more broadly: "In their partial and allusive imitation, parodies talk back to their sources, their very existence announcing that modern art is a conversation—and not just a conversation between works of art, but between different works of art, their social contexts, and their readers."[2] Hastings uses her knack for imitation to push for a criticism that is dialogic and empathetic.

Throughout the exchange, Pound situates his responses as part of a larger project. He uses numbered titles—"The Approach to Paris—I"; "The Approach to Paris—II"; and so on until the seventh and concluding section. Hastings titles her essays based on the elements of Pound's essays to which she is most directly responding. Her first essay, published on September 18, 1913 in response to Pound's first two "Approach to Paris" essays, is called "The Way Back to America." On September 25, *The New Age* publishes "The Clear Tongue Plus Pindarism;" on October 2, "Humanititism and the New Form;" on October 9, "Aristophanes or Tailharde." The final Hastings essay, "All Against Anything," appears in the same October 16 issue as Pound's conclusion. Hastings signals in her titles an equal familiarity with ancient Greeks and modern manifesto writers. She also shows her interest in acknowledging what's been presented in the conversation so far, something that Pound does occasionally and begrudgingly.

Their verbal brawl took place in a British journal called *The New Age*.[3] Founded in 1907, the journal was funded by George Bernard Shaw as an organ of the Christian socialist reform group The Fabian Society. Holbrook Jackson and Hastings's lover and collaborator A.R. Orage shared editing duties for the journal's first year, with Orage staying in that role through 1922. Hastings played a central role in soliciting, responding to, and editing writing for the journal. In a score-settling autobiographical pamphlet written in 1936, Hastings claimed, "I had to fight not only Orage, but the whole office, to get Pound's articles in at all. They were so idiosyncratic that I did not trust my own judgment, and I read them out; and everyone howled. However, I put them through."[4] Though Pound's articles may have seemed ridiculous even to the journal's own editors, their inclusion was par for the course in this period of particularly raucous dialogue in *The New Age*.[5] Editors, including Hastings, frequently solicited writing that opposed the central principles of the editorial staff.[6] They sought "outspoken and controversial new contributors," whether or not they had any interest in the tenets of guild socialism.[7]

One way that regular contributors talked back to the guest writers in their journal was through parody. Several features engaged in mocking imitations, including the regular column titled "Pastiche," letters to the editor, and one-off columns. In her discussion of Katherine Mansfield's *New Age* parodies co-written with Hastings, Carey Snyder notes that parody has an "ambivalent status at *The New Age*"; it appeared frequently within the journal, but often in the less prestigious sections of the publication.[8] Hastings enthusiastically participates in *The New Age* project through her imitations, parodies, and translations. Moreover, she elevates the status of parody in the magazine by engaging with one of the most important critics of the period. With the T.K.L. essays of Beatrice Hastings, *The New Age* participates in a transatlantic trend: the lampooning of modernist language in modern periodicals.[9] Parody has a flexible and varied purpose among these publications: newspaper parodies can bemoan the loss of conventional artistic and moral standards, while "smart" magazines like *Vanity Fair* use the same strategies to grant their readers a blasé sophistication.[10] But in the late nineteenth and early twentieth centuries, it most often serves the purpose that we see in *The New Age*: mimicking the textual qualities of modernist writing while at the same time establishing how the parodist holds a more common-sense view of what constitutes art.[11] The parodies, translations, and imitations in the T.K.L. essays participate in just such a dual move. Snyder observes that *The New Age* "parodies articulate a set of aesthetic values in a comic rather than polemic mode."[12] In the case of Hastings's debate with Pound, the move from explanation into parody often marks a particularly polemic mode, one where her feelings about poetry are so strongly felt that she has to show instead of tell.

Dialogue and parody destabilized the positions taken by the magazine, as did the absence of clear credit to identifiable authors. Submissions in *The New Age* could appear in "signed, anonymous, and pseudonymous" forms, making it particularly difficult to assign consistent positions to the contributors.[13] If pseudonyms and parody were among the most common strategies in the journal, Beatrice Hastings was the master of both. Hastings proudly claims contributions to *The New Age* "in a dozen various styles under different pseudonyms and anonymously."[14] Hastings writes about the ways that her embrace of a number of pseudonyms meant the loss of her own artistic authority:

> My present-day friends, accustomed to the push and publicity of this period, find it hard to understand how I could be so disastrously indifferent to claiming my work; how I could go on, year after year, writing anonymously or under pseudonyms that allowed readers to set down my work to other people, mainly to Orage. Puzzle or no (I could explain it with more space; I thought it better for the paper) there it is. I did so. I cared for nothing but the paper, that was my life.[15]

Among a number of two- and three-letter initials, she also used pen names such as Pagan, Alice Morning, Mrs. Malaprop, Beatrice

Tina, D. Triformis, and G. Whiz.[16] Her *New Age* pen names give a sense of her style, her learnedness, and her sense of humor. The pseudonym that Hastings used in her debates with Pound, T.K.L., seems neutral enough by comparison (though neutrality can be gendered; Pound mistook her identity for that of a man when he responded to the first parodic essay). She had used the pen-name T.K.L. extensively in a wide variety of previous writings for the journal, from poems to book reviews to humorous recaps of court cases. A pseudonym without many clear associations may have been particularly useful because it enabled her to take on additional voices in her essays: she channels Pound's slangy intellectualism and shifts easily into the style of the French poets she translates and imitates. Since boxing was popular among intellectuals in the 1910's and '20s, though, perhaps we should hear in T.K.L. an echo of "TKO," a technical knockout.[17]

Where Pound uses his essay series as an opportunity to solidify his reputation as an authority on the avant-garde, Hastings uses a pseudonymous voice to speak for the collective: for the English literary tradition that Pound dismisses wholesale, for the self-educated *New Age* readers who may not understand his untranslated poetry, and for the editorial voice of the magazine as a whole. Critics of *The New Age* marvel at the breadth of Hastings's pseudonymous writing. Her polyvocality suggests that we need new frameworks for understanding authorial voice.[18] This exchange with Pound highlights the ways that pseudonyms, parody, and translation all work together in her essays. All three strategies disavow and complicate the connection between author and text. They push back against the publicity-based and personality-based strategies of the modernist avant-gardes.

Though Pound's ostensible aim in the "Approach to Paris" essays is to introduce English audiences to modern French poetry, the point of view that he takes throughout is a resolutely personal, even solipsistic one. The essays return to a few key poetic criteria, none of which will surprise readers familiar with Pound's aesthetic.

He regularly praises poems for their experiments in rhythm and assonance, their clarity and simplicity, and their engagement with modern life, all values for which he argues so forcefully in "A Few Don'ts by an Imagiste," published in *Poetry* earlier that same year. But these markers of aesthetic consistency often get lost since Pound takes pains to emphasize the idiosyncrasy of his choices. "It is hopeless to speak in general terms," he says in the first essay, "the voyager can but tell his private adventures; so be it."[19] Throughout the rest of the essays, Pound defends his conception of poetry as a private experience between the text and reader. Hastings imagines quite a different model of poetry: one that is written for the public, translatable into different forms and languages, inherently mediated by convention and history; it's part of a tradition, one might say, rather than evidence of an individual talent. She argues for the importance of this understanding chiefly through a writing style that emphasizes imitative and public language. Translation, parody, and other second-order linguistic moves are central to Hastings's repertoire. They serve as mimetic devices that both explain and undercut the pretensions of the avant-garde, particularly those that mystify personal aesthetic experience and claim that it is unexplainable.

The back-and-forth between Pound and Hastings shows how the periodical press makes this new kind of author function possible; it also shows the difficulty of extracting it from its original publication context. Pound's essays epitomize the typical understanding of the author in this era: they are internally consistent, attached to a biographical identity, and written in the main in order to generate a sense of their author as an arbiter of taste. They are extractable from the conversation, and indeed they have been anthologized as stand-alone essays.[20] T.K.L.'s essays, by contrast are more dependent on the context of the conversation. Although her essay "The Way Back to America" is included in the anthology *Gender and Modernism*, some of her turns of phrase lose their piquancy when we don't see what they're imitating.[21]

I'll take a moment to compare one of Pound's turns of phrase and Hastings's imitation of it. Hastings dissects Pound's prose style throughout this series of essays, so this is only one representative sample. When Pound lists several stanzas of Remy de Gourmont's "Rose" poem, he stops with the claim "And so it runs with ever more sweeping cadence with ever more delicate accords, and if you are not too drunk with the sheer naming over of beauty you will wake at the end of the reading and know that the procession of all women that ever were has passed before you."[22] Pound wants the reader to be swept away by Gourmont's catalog of "roses," so he carries on the anaphora in his description, repeating the phrase "with ever more." But in the second half of the clause he reframes our perceptions—these are not mere flowers Gourmont has been describing, but women. In her essay, Hastings skewers Pound's decadent view of being transported by poetry, his tic of repetition, and his sexism: "If you are not too drunk with the delicate stuff to be able to carry it as if, as if, I repeat, unconcerned, you will wake at the end of the reading to know that the pageant of all the subtle, neglected, misunderstood poets that ever were has passed before you." So instead of waking from the dream created by the poem, in this instance you wake at the end of the reading because it has put you to sleep. Instead of carrying on a gentle rhythm with her repetitions, Hastings calls attention to them and interrupts the flow of her thought. But most damning to Pound is the move from "the procession of all women that ever were" to "the pageant of all the subtle, neglected, misunderstood poets that ever were." Hastings moves from the imagined (boring, sexist) archetypal flow of images to a more specific set, one specifically tailored to the identity of her interlocutor. Instead of a parade of his ideal object, the poem is a mirror showing him himself over and over. Because each of Hastings's essays responds so directly to the phrasing of the previous Pound essay, one can only appreciate the extent of her wit and mimicry when they're read side-by-side.

From the first paragraph of her initial response essay "The Way Back to America," Hastings not only imitates Pound; she imagines dialogue interrupting her imitative voice:

> Attendez, mes enfants! I am about to waste ten minutes in exposition of the so-called English poets. What I have to say is brief, pardieu! They were all French! Who is that interrupting? Ha—you wish to infer that Chaucer wrote no poetry until he forgot he had once been in France? Well, you may infer what you please, I suppose. What? The 'Canterbury Tales'? I smile explosively—all pure French, my dear sir! Now sit down and let me talk.

Hastings creates a Pound-like voice and highlights the fake sophistication of the original. Through the use of French words, exclamations, and one quasi-futurist poetic phrase—"I smile explosively"—she skewers the author as a slavish literary hipster, one beholden to the latest innovations from the continent. His modishness seems to go hand-in-hand with an impatience for conversation. T.K.L.'s implied speaker immediately dismisses anyone who might question his counterintuitive claim that the English poets are French. Instead of engaging in a Socratic dialogue, he insists that the silent interlocutor "sit down and let me talk." With the flexibility of her voice, Hastings forces a conversation when Pound would prefer a serial monologue.

Translation serves as one major flashpoint in this series of essays. One would not think it would be such a contentious topic, since both Hastings and Pound regularly translated poetry for *The New Age*.[23] Ann Ardis has identified the ways that Pound shows disdain toward his audience and abdicates his responsibilities as a critic by failing to translate or fully explain his choices.[24] In some respects, though, we can see this choice as part of Pound's overall refusal to engage in the kind of derivative or second-order speech you need to do in order to rewrite. And since Pound's "approach" focuses on poetry's musicality more than its content, his decision to quote large chunks of poetry in their original language seems to assert that the rhythm and assonance of the poetry would be lost in translation. He's in good company: Charles Baudelaire's "Correspondences" and Arthur Rimbaud's "Vowels" make similar claims about poetic sound communicating beyond the register of linguistic comprehension, as do T.S. Eliot's essays about Dante. Hastings, however, finds this to be mystifying nonsense.[25] In this respect, she follows contemporaneous popular critiques of Anglo-American modernism, which use parody to highlight the elitism and decadence of the new art's investment in "difficulty" as an aesthetic.[26] She compares a stanza of the Remy de Gourmont piece quoted at length in Pound's "Approach to Paris—II," both in its original and translated forms. "In French," she says, "the thing is a marvel," while in English the poetry sounds nonsensical, like the language of a madman.[27]

For Hastings, translating a poem into English unmasks the poetic pretensions of the original that would otherwise remain hidden behind the mystical veneer of rolled rs and nasal ns. Most often in the case of Pound's poets, this pretension can be characterized as a desire to throw out any stable meanings or definitions in favor of unstable, evocative linguistic play. The "pure poetry" of the French modernists, then, prefigures a Derridean postmodernism. In "The Way Back to America," she jokes that the "ineffable words" of her brother poet "mean anything you like, cows, roses, toads, dairymaids, or queens—if you *must* have a meaning, but why have one?"[28] We're venturing into the absurdist territory of *Through the Looking-Glass* here, where Humpty Dumpty claims that a word means whatever he chooses it to mean. The same outrage at new writers who toss all stable meanings out the window comes through in her later joke about a poet writing a series of poetic genres "in prose," to be followed by a second series of prose genres (the novel, the essay, the encyclopedia) "in poesie": "You see, friends, if we can only mix everything up and break every law of the common aesthetic, it will be much better for the trade."[29] As Pound admits in a later discussion of translation, many of the issues that he places in the aesthetic realm also belong in the economic one. This is particularly clear in "Approach to Paris—IV" when he collapses the desire to maintain an unmediated poetic experience with the desire to adhere to copyright law.

Through her translations and parodies, Hastings pushes Pound to define his terms and explain his strategies. Though he does translate some of Charles Vildrac's poetry in "Approach to Paris—III," the essay that shares space in the same issue as "The Way Back to America," he responds more directly to Hastings's issues with translation in the fourth installment. Working his way through a Jules Romains poem with a combination of explanatory introduction, quotation, and translation, he says, "Such, in rough outline, is the 'Ode à la foule qui est ici.' I have naturally lost all semblance of the original sweep and of the original sound, partly because the translation rights are reserved and there is not time to write for permission to break them, partly because I do not wish to interpose a pretentious translation between the reader and the easily obtainable original."[30] What was implicit about Pound's rhetorical choices from the beginning has been made explicit only because Hastings mocked them and showed the alternatives. As a consequence of this imagined unmediated encounter, Pound doesn't want to imitate or represent the poem in a new language. Perhaps the most striking element of his excuse, though, is the claim that he doesn't want to violate the established contractual terms for translating the poem as a whole. Here it's the literary marketplace, and not the skill of the author, that interferes with the creation of a proper translation.[31]

The bravura moment where Hastings translates in order to repudiate comes in her third essay, "Humanititism and the New Form." (As with her repeated misspelling of Tailhade as

Tailharde in the following essay, Hastings's addition of a syllable to Pound's term "Humanitism" seems to be a subtle jab, though it could just be a typo.) This essay responds to Pound's full, and sometimes pained translation of another Charles Vildrac poem, "The Visit." Pound had qualified his translation in a number of ways: he tells us that this is "a rough prose version," and highlights the few places where words and phrases are idiomatic or "untranslatable."[32] Hastings makes no falsely-modest excuses; instead, she tells her readers that she has made a change to the poem in translation for their benefit: "In English, needless to say, the Prosie comes out somewhat flat, but by substituting the first personal pronoun for Vildrac's third, you will find the thing lift a bit." She then spends more than a full column of her two and a half column essay re-presenting a poem that Pound has already fully presented in translation.

Why does Hastings spend so many column inches re-translating a boring poem about an unpleasant character? She does so, I suggest, in order to bring together her critiques of literary mystification, realistic language, and the narcissism of contemporary writers. "The Visit" sits somewhere between translation and parody: it is not so over the top in its effects as the "Cow" parody of Remy de Gourmont in "The Way Back to America," but it is flat and repetitive enough to highlight what Hastings sees as the narrator's moral failings:

> But suddenly I thought of Jones,
> And felt sad and also somewhat annoyed.
> For he symbolises my broken promises.
> I shuddered to think I thought of Jones.
>
> I think I thought of Jones to shudder.
> I love to feel myself feeling.

Hastings skewers the poetically-minded speaker for his unremarkable sense of himself as a remarkable person. Other people seem to exist only to present him with further opportunities to interrogate his own stream of consciousness. It's not a stretch to imagine this narrator as analogous to Pound, whose chief criterion for lauding Francis Jammes in a later essay seems to be that he reminds Pound of his own pleasant memories of travel.[33] Indeed, Hastings suspects that not just Pound but "every minor poet in London" will recognize the selfish and aestheticized view of human relations presented by Vildrac. Since neither the language nor the verse form is complex, they will be able to translate it as well. She imagines the kind of desire for self-transformation and interpersonal connection that good poetry evokes in its readers, and then imagines the way that Vildrac's poem short-circuits that desire: "You have the impulse to go out and experience a new sensation; fulfil your word! Don't take so much trouble! Just read and translate Vildrac's "Visite"—then you will believe you have actually *done* the thing."[34]

Looking at the ways translation and parody are interwoven throughout this exchange, we can see Hastings not only making a claim about the poetry Pound is presenting but a related critique about the solipsism of the artistic perspective he champions. Translation and parody both facilitate dialogue and as such they enable other forms of interpretation than the purely self-involved ones. She uses her "English talent for adopting" to translate Pound from the avant-gardese, bringing his ideas about free verse and realism to a broader readership even as she eviscerates many of them. Particularly since the inception of the Modernist Journals Project, literary critics have a much clearer sense of how contentious and diverse were the responses to modernism in the magazines. A focus on parody and translation as related strategies brings Hastings more fully into current conversations about modernist parody and the periodical press.

NOTES

1. Ezra Pound, "Letter to the Editor: 'The Approach to Paris,'" *The New Age*, September 25, 1913, 647.

2. Leonard Diepeveen, *Mock Modernism: An Anthology of Parodies, Travesties, Frauds, 1910-1935*. (Toronto: University of Toronto Press, 2014), 11.

3. *The New Age* has become an important part of recent modernist literary study in part because of its early inclusion in the Modernist Journals Project. Robert Scholes gives an overview of the journal's history and editorial in his "General Introduction to *The New Age*, 1907-1922," Modernist Journals Project, accessed July 21, 2015, http://modjourn.org. The first and most extensive scholarly examination of the journal's history is Wallace Martin, *The New Age Under Orage: Chapters in English Cultural History*. (Manchester: Manchester University Press; New York: Barnes & Noble, 1967).

4. Beatrice Hastings, *The Old "New Age": Orage and Others* (London: Blue Moon Press, 1936), 6.

5. The contested, conversational quality of *The New Age* has featured prominently in the critical discussion of it. Though she does identify the journal as socialist at its heart, Ann Ardis emphasizes the journal's valuing of dialogue, particularly from critics of avant-garde modernism such as Beatrice Hastings. See "The Dialogics of Modernism(s) in the New Age," *Modernism/modernity* 14:3 (2007): 407–34 and *Modernism and Cultural Conflict, 1880-1922*, (Cambridge, U.K.; New York: Cambridge University Press, 2002). Lee Garver suggests that we should understand *The New Age* more in terms of its oppositionality than any particular political points of view that it holds as a journal. See Lee Garver. "Neither Progressive nor Reactionary: Reassessing the Cultural Politics of The New Age." *The Journal of Modern Periodical Studies* 2:1 (2011): 86–115.

6. Lee Garver, "Neither Progressive nor Reactionary: Reassessing the Cultural Politics of *The New Age*," *The Journal of Modern Periodical Studies* 2:1 (2011): 102–3.

7. Ibid., 107.

8. Carey Snyder, "Katherine Mansfield and the *New Age* School of Satire," *The Journal of Modern Periodical Studies* 1:2 (2010): 142.

9. The scholar most engaged with the practice of modernist parody is Leonard Diepeveen. See his *The Difficulties of Modernism* (New York: Routledge, 2002) and the introduction to *Mock Modernism: An Anthology of Parodies, Travesties, Frauds, 1910-1935* (Toronto: University of Toronto Press, 2014). Carey Snyder discusses Hastings and Katherine Mansfield co-writing a parody for *The New Age* in Snyder, "Katherine Mansfield and the New Age School of Satire." Though it does not discuss *The New Age* directly, Daniel Tracy has influenced many of my claims with his "Investing in 'Modernism': Smart

Magazines, Parody, and Middlebrow Professional Judgment," *The Journal of Modern Periodical Studies* 1:1 (2010): 38–63.

10. "Parodies offer the reader a sense of sophistication because they both teach the object parodied and deny the reader ever needed to be taught." Daniel Tracy, "Investing in 'Modernism,'" 53.

11. Diepeveen, *Mock Modernism*, 13.

12. Snyder, "Katherine Mansfield and the New Age School of Satire," 130.

13. Ardis, "The Dialogics of Modernism(s) in the New Age," 416

14. Hastings, *The Old "New Age,"* 3.

15. Ibid., 7–8.

16. For a discussion of these pen names and more, see Robert Scholes, "Hastings, Beatrice (Emily Alice Haigh) (1879-1943)," Modernist Journals Project, accessed July 21, 2015, http://modjourn.org.

17. Ann Ardis's evocative description of Pound and Hastings engaging in "bouts of verbal puglilism" undoubtedly inspired this phrase, if only subconsciously. "The Dialogics of Modernism(s) in *The New Age*," 420.

18. Ann Ardis argues that Hastings "playfully and deliberately violated every convention of the author function that is commonly upheld in literary studies." "The Dialogics of Modernism(s) in *The New Age*," 430. Sean Latham suggests that Hastings is among many women modernists whose work on periodicals "requires us to develop new models for thinking about authorship, identity, and cultural history from within the mess and muddle of periodical culture more generally." "The Mess and Muddle of Modernism: The Modernist Journals Project and Modern Periodical Studies," *Tulsa Studies in Women's Literature* 30:2 (2011): 410.

19. Ezra Pound, "The Approach to Paris—I," *The New Age*, September 4, 1913, 551.

20. See for instance, "The Approach to Paris" in *Ezra Pound, Selected Prose, 1909-1965* (New York: New Directions, 1975), 363-373.

21. Beatrice Hastings, "The Way Back to America" in Bonnie Kime Scott, *Gender in Modernism: New Geographies, Complex Intersections* (Champaign, IL: University of Illinois Press, 2007), 178-181.

22. Ezra Pound, "The Approach to Paris—II," *The New Age*, September 11, 1913, 578.

23. As Wallace Martin observes in *The New Age Under Orage*, "Pound's first contribution to the magazine was his translation of 'The Seafarer,'" followed by translations of Provencal poetry, 175-176.

24. Ardis, "The Dialogics of Modernism(s) in the New Age," 415.

25. Hastings continues to chide Pound for his mystifying tendencies. In a later essay, she responds to his claims about vorticism by calling him "a hopeless cultist" and comparing him to a fortune-teller. See Alice Morning, "Impressions of Paris," *The New Age*, January 21, 1915, 308–9.

26. See *The Difficulties of Modernism*, especially chapter 1, "Difficulty as Fashion," 1-42.

27. T.K.L. (Beatrice Hastings), "The Way Back to America," *The New Age*, September 8, 1913, 605.

28. Ibid.

29. Ibid.

30. Ezra Pound, "The Approach to Paris—IV," *The New Age*, September 25, 1913, 631.

31. Of course, Pound was beholden to the marketplace himself. As Hastings observes, "Pound had to be *paid*." Hastings, *The Old "New Age*," 7.

32. Pound, "The Approach to Paris—IV," 631, 632.

33. Ezra Pound, "The Approach to Paris—VI," *The New Age*, October 9, 1913, 695.

34. T.K.L. (Beatrice Hastings), "Humanititism and the New Form," *The New Age*, October 2, 1913, 669.

"A MINOR POET OF THE FIRST CLASS"

Benjamin Johnson

BENJAMIN JOHNSON *is an associate professor at the University of Central Missouri. His articles on modern poetry and culture have appeared in venues including* Texas Studies in Literature and Language, Arizona Quarterly, *and* The Wallace Stevens Journal.

THE last fifteen years have seen a small-but-steady uptick of scholarly interest in the largely forgotten early-twentieth-century writer Beatrice Hastings. However, this scholarship has focused primarily on Hastings's prose: biographer Stephen Gray writes mostly about her memoirs and loosely-veiled biographical fiction; Ann Ardis and Lucy Delap examine her political essays; Carey Snyder looks at Hastings's satirical collaborations with Katherine Mansfield; and Robert Scholes focuses on her essay series "Impressions of Paris." And so Hastings, whose poetry appeared regularly in *The New Age*, and who was referred to by Max Jacob shortly after her 1914 arrival in Paris as "an authentic great English poet,"[1] has continued to be ignored as a poet even as increasing attention has been paid to her essays and literary fiction.

Hastings's poetry has been especially obscure because her poems have never been collected into a book. She published a significant number of poems—from roughly 1909 to 1913, she generally published at least one poem a month, and often quite a bit more than that, and she continued to publish poems with slightly less frequency during and after the First World War.[2] She certainly wrote enough poetry to fill a small collection, but she focused her first efforts at book publication on prose, which in the early years of her career resulted in *Woman's Worst Enemy: Woman*, a 1909 collection of essays about the sexual and domestic lives of women, and a 1911 novella entitled *The Maid's Comedy*. Hastings seems to have seen her poetry as a secondary concern in which she took a great deal of pride: she joked in 1913 that "The humorous truth about me has become quite clear to myself whatever the conception of others may be. I am a minor poet of the first class."[3]

The best of Hastings's poetry is worth rediscovering, not least because the best of it is quite good. She is no great formal innovator, but she is a strong practitioner of traditional prosody, and she is quite cunning at using classical motifs to investigate modern sexual and political life. Moreover, her poems add important shadings to studies of her career that have focused primarily on her essays and fiction. Hastings's prose is sharp, funny, and incisive, but it is not usually overtly sexual. Hastings writes in the introduction to *Woman's Worst Enemy: Woman* that her book will denounce "the sort of woman whose modesty howls for silence on such important matters as sex and maternity", but it is only in her poetry that Hastings goes beyond just denouncing silence about sexuality to depict scenes of sensual abandon and domestic rebellion. In part because of this, Hastings's poetry strikes me as being her most feminist writing. In her prose voices, Hastings is often bluntly anti-feminist, especially in her attacks on the suffrage movement under the pseudonym D. Triformis, and negative comments about women's creative and intellectual capacity recur across Hastings's various pseudonyms. In her poems, however, she repeatedly deploys female speakers who are rebellious, anti-patriarchal, and tauntingly sexual. These poems are thus vital to understanding the full range of Hastings's many voices.

Her poems are also worth reading for what they add to modernist studies—*The New Age*, after all, was publishing these poems alongside work by writers like Hulme, Flint, and Pound, and if Hastings was not as formally audacious as the leading lights of the modernist avant-garde, she was nevertheless looking for her own ways to "make it new." Hastings reminds me of H.D. with her clever repurposing of characters from classical literature, and her interest in sexual expression is obviously of a piece with what Loy was doing in the same time period. Hastings is not as good a poet as H.D. or Loy, but her work demonstrates that poetry which challenged gender norms was not the sole province of the free-versifying avant-garde during the 1910's.

Hastings's own favorite poem was "The Lost Bacchante." Even John Carswell, who argues in his 1978 study of *The New Age* group that "when [Hastings] tried to write poetry it was a disastrous failure,"[4] thought that "The Lost Bacchante" was a notable exception.[5] The poem exemplifies one of the main interests of Hastings's poetry, namely the refiguration and dramatization of female mythological figures. A bacchante is a priestess of Bacchus, and the bacchante in this poem is "lost" in the sense that the bacchanal has moved on without her. The followers of Bacchus have been up to no good, "cursing the rite" of a maid who had prayed in vain for help with a recalcitrant lover, but the lost bacchante decides to get revenge on her fellow priestesses by "blessing the rite" of this "mortal maid" in stanza three.[6] The last three stanzas of the poem are delightfully energetic, beginning with the lost bacchante's jarring declaration that "I'll tear me a robe from a tiger's spine." She binds her hair in vine tendrils, which seems a mighty bacchanalian thing to do, and then proceeds to "the city, / Where the mortals dance to-night" in stanza five. Setting the conclusion of the poem in a city is a surprising and modernizing choice, since you would expect to find a follower of Bacchus in a more sylvan setting. Once she is in the city, Hastings's lost bacchante wrenches "pity" out of the breast of the man the maid loves, and replaces it with "mad delight."

In the final stanza, the lost bacchante does far more than that. She declares in the first line of the final stanza that "I'll work in the milky heart of the maid." Suddenly, it is not just the lover who is being manipulated, but also the maid herself whose heart is being worked upon. But why is her heart "milky?" Milky breasts or bosoms are a truism, but a milky heart is unusual. Hastings perhaps indicates that the milk-white purity of the maid reaches even to her heart, though I suspect she also means to imply that the maid is a bit boring. The milk in the maid's heart might also be associated with motherhood, and here it should be noted that Hastings frequently attacked the idea that women naturally desire to be mothers.[7] Her 1909 book *Woman's Worst Enemy: Woman* opens with a critique of the cult of maternity, and her introduction culminates with this declaration: "To my youthful disgust at the idea of childbirth, I add a conclusion: Never have I seen the adult creature of whom I would like to be the mother." The lost bacchante, for her part, seeks to overcome the pure or maternal milkiness of the maid by using her bacchanalian magic to "ripen" the maid's "bosom scanty." A ripened bosom could also be associated with maternity, of course, but at least in this stanza the focus of that ripening is entirely in the service of erotic possession—possession by the lover who clasps the mortal maid, but also possession by the lost bacchante who in the final lines seems to have overtaken the maid's subjectivity. Significantly, the second line of the final stanza—"with magic I'll ripen her bosom scanty"—departs from the established rhythmic pattern of the poem. The poem had previously been in regular common meter—4, 3, 4, 3—but here the second line of the stanza has four stresses. Rhythm overflows the poem at the precise moment when desire overtakes the maid and she is possessed by the bacchante's magic.

Possession here is obviously a metaphor for desire itself—an urge or demiurge that disrupts subjectivity—but given that Hastings was so concerned in this period of her career with thinking about gender norms, I also find it persuasive to read the poem as a mockery of a tendency in some men toward what Freud, just two years later, would call "psychical impotence." You, gentle reader, might know this condition by its more popular name: the "Madonna-whore complex." As Freud describes it, "the whole sphere of love in such people remains divided in the two directions personified in art as sacred and profane (or animal) love. Where they love they do not desire, and where they desire they cannot love."[8] We can guess from the beginning of Hastings's poem, when the maid is performing a "rite" to attract her "loved one," that her attempts to curry his favor by more ordinary means have probably failed. The lover might respect the maid in the same way that Freud's subject might respect a Madonna-figure, but it is clear in the early stanzas that he does not desire her. It is only in the final stanza, when the maid is possessed and transformed by the tendril-clad bacchante, that we see the male lover "gasp" and "clasp."

Here it is worth recalling how violent the poem is throughout—there is a trampling in stanza two; open wounds in stanza three; and the aforementioned tiger-skinning in stanza four. This violence can obviously be read as representing the disordering power of sexual desire, but it might also suggest the drastic subjective shifts that are necessary if an individual woman is going to attempt to embody both Madonna and whore—or, in Hastings's terms, if she is going to be a milky-hearted maid who also has a side of her personality which is willing and able to flay a tiger. The male lover in the final stanza unwittingly gets to have his cake and eat it—one way to read the conclusion is as a sort of magical ménage-a-trois—but the joke is that only the lost bacchante actually knows what is happening. The poem, then, is a celebration feminine sexual control, but it also functions quite powerfully as a lampooning of the lengths a woman must go to if she wants simultaneously to be maidenly enough to be respected and exciting enough to be desired.

Hastings also uses classical motifs as a way to think about sexual abandon in her poem "Metamorphosis," particularly in the second half of the poem. The poem is spoken by a woman—a bacchante named Chloe—whom an "Apollonian enchanter" has turned into a sheep.[9] In the first half of the poem, she asks her companions if they recognize her, but they seem not to because she is, as previously mentioned, a sheep. In the second half of the poem, Chloe begs to be liberated from her metamorphosed form, and Hastings energizes the lines by threading command verbs into the beats of two pounding lines written primarily in dactylic trimeter: "Thrust me back, tear from this carcase / Wool, skin, horns—all that disguises." Most obviously, the poem is about a desire to be liberated from a false identity, and Chloe specifically asks other women to tear away her covering to reveal her "white limbs." Chloe's desires are both orgiastic and homoerotic, and Hastings also layers a great deal of deflowering imagery into the poem in lines like "Seeing this blood blush the thicket" and "Tear me, ye tender nurses! / With beautiful hands break asunder." "Metamorphosis" resembles "The Lost Bacchante" in that it builds to a sexually and rhetorically intense conclusion, but where the speaker of "The Lost Bacchante" is almost mockingly in control in the final stanzas, Chloe begs for a moment of ecstatic, transformative abandon. In both poems, though, Hastings includes a character who is a symbol of purity—a maid, a lamb—and suggests that purity is just a disguise waiting to be burst through by transgressive desire

"Vashti" is also a poem about transgression, but here the transgression is a direct refusal of patriarchal power. In the Book of Esther, Vashti is the wife of King Ahasuerus, and when she refuses his command to dance for his banquet guests, she is replaced as queen. Hastings's version of the story is notable for its focus on fear. Vashti knows if she runs from the palace that "Kings' horses halt never," and she also knows that "men may enter this chamber/ Singing me forth to die."[10] Moreover, she knows that these men will ensure that in the future no one will "dare remember/ My name was Vashti." It is poignant that in Hastings's rendition of this tale, Vashti's greatest fear is that she will be unsung. However, immediately after her expression of fear, Vashti recalls that "To-night I am Queen. See the blue, green and white, / The tassels all golden, / And silk cords purple." The poem had not previously used any words related to color, but suddenly it has five in the space of three lines as the poem builds to its final stanza, where Vashti lays out a feminist call to arms— perhaps the clearest such call in any of Hastings's writing—as she asks women to join her in a "Banquet of Freedom!"

A similar ethic of principled refusal characterizes "In The Presence," which strikes me as a more complicated version of the ideas explored in "Vashti." Hastings begins each stanza by asking "To whom should I confess?"[11] and then rejects various authorities that might hear her confession. In the first stanza, the speaker refuses to confess to a Priest. She notes punningly that her "early prayer / Lies yet" upon an altar, and also states that while she might once have been able to bring hope, innocence, and faith to a priest, that is not an option in "this later year." In the second stanza, the speaker rejects romanticism. She could go tell her tale to nature, and she is tempted by the "giddy heights" of sublimity, but she also knows that these heights will "cast her down." Shelley in particular seems to be invoked in this stanza, with its heights and songbirds, but the speaker suggests that the fascination with self-destruction that is built into the sublime is something she has pursued before but does not wish to pursue again. In the third stanza, the speaker has no interest in confessing to the men who would fling a "timid, bigot stone" due to a desire to fit in with the mob. And then in the fourth stanza, things get interesting. The speaker wonders if she should confess to her own soul, and describes herself alone with "the clean sand / Whereon I write, with unabsolving hand, / My sin—and next, the new vows I have made." The imagery here is fascinating—even when confessing only to herself, the speaker writes in sand, presumably ensuring that the confession will wash away with the tide. Moreover, her hand is unabsolving, and indeed she seems uninterested in absolution. She writes her sin, but does not express remorse, and implies that her sin is no great matter since its mark is only temporary. Her new vows are also temporary, since they are written only to be washed away. The reader can't help but wonder if the violation of these new vows will be the next sin which she will confess to the "clean sand" of her soul. Here, in her playful unwillingness to apologize for herself, Hastings reminds me more than a little bit of Millay, another formally inclined poet whom scholars of modernism were quite happy to overlook for decades. The poem begins by refusing various calcified modes of masculine authority, and ends by celebrating an utterly malleable vision of the self. The soul is the only authority to whom the speaker will confess, perhaps because the soul and the self are both, in this image, in a perpetual state of remaking themselves.

The last poem I want to talk about is "Mind Pictures," a proto-imagist attempt to describe figures the speaker says she has "seen in instant flashes."[12] The first five lines of the poem are incredibly lovely:

> The brown-skinned boy asleep beneath a clump
> Of red-spiked aloe, red the flower;
> > A mighty stream, moon flooded, meeting ocean
> > Between two crags which box the encounter
> > Of the majestic waters.

If you isolate the first five lines, you have a modernist poem—Hastings focuses on a single image, her language is austere, and she takes some liberties with grammar.[13] I suspect that many readers seeing this compressed, seaside vignette might think of Moore's "The Fish" or H.D.'s *Sea Garden*. In line six, though, Hastings does what the modernist avant-garde often does not: she gives us a key to explicate the poem: "What others have I seen in instant flashes?" She thus tells us that the figures in the poem are, as she puts it in the title, "mind pictures," or images which have flashed through her mind. Significantly, all three of the humans she depicts in the poem are, in one way or another, marginalized: a brown-skinned boy; a woman fleeing shame; a beggar. The poem is a sort of triptych of the oppressed, and the final three lines are especially powerful: "A beggar, catching shell-fish from a rock, / With nought for all the world to covet, / Nor kith nor kin nor ox nor ass nor anything." Hastings seems, with her "instant flashes" and her brutalist parade of "nor," to be groping toward the sensibilities that will come to define the early years of English-language modernism, but there is not the least bit of art for art's sake here. This is art for the sake of outrage. The poem as a whole is mostly written in loose pentameter, but in the final line, Hastings's rhythm becomes absolutely rigid for four beats—"Nor kith nor kin nor ox nor ass"—but then refuses to resolve itself pleasantly into a final iamb, as she concludes with "nor anything," thus appending not one but two unstressed syllables onto the end of the line. Hastings begins her poem with some of her most beautiful writing, and ends it in a moment of intentional rhythmic brutality which underscores her political critique of human brutality.

I believe that Hastings's self-assessment was fairly spot-on: she is a minor poet of the first class. Her work has been forgotten for a number of reasons—she had bad luck with publishers, her best writing was in periodicals rather than books, her use of pseudonyms makes her writing difficult to locate, and she made more than her share of enemies. Some current trends in modernist studies—most notably the increased interest in modern periodicals—bode well for some resuscitation of Hastings's reputation. If that happens, I definitely think that these poems— these passionate, funny, sexy, prosodically complicated poems— should be a vital part of the story of Hastings's career.

NOTES

1. Quoted in Jeffrey Meyers, *Modigliani: A Life* (London: Gerald Duckworth & Co., 2006), 138.

2. Her poems appear under a variety of her pseudonyms. In her early years at *The New Age*, most of her poems were published under her "literary" pseudonyms Beatrice Tina and Beatrice Hastings, and later she published satirical verse as T.K.L., and more serious pieces under her "Impressions of Paris" pseudonym Alice Morning.

3. Beatrice Hastings, "Two Reviews," *The New Age*, October 23,1913, 759.

4. John Carswell, *Lives and Letters: A. R. Orage, Beatrice Hastings, Katherine Mansfield, John Middleton Murry, S. S. Koteliansky, 1906-1957* (New York: New Directions, 1978), 30.

5. For a more recent dismissal of Hastings's poetic abilities, see Meyers, 138.

6. Beatrice Hastings, "The Lost Bacchante," *The New Age*, June 9, 1910, 124.

7. See Erin Kingsley's article in this book for a more thorough examination of Hastings's writing on maternity.

8. Sigmund Freud, "On the Universal Tendency to Debasement in the Sphere of Love," in *The Freud Reader* (New York: W.W. Norton and Co., 1989), 397.

9. Beatrice Tina, "Metamorphosis," *The New Age*, December 10, 1908, 133.

10. Beatrice Tina, "Vashti," *The New Age*, November 25, 1909, 76.

11. Beatrice Hastings, "In the Presence," *The New Age*, September 15, 1910, 462.

12. Beatrice Tina, "Mind Pictures," *The New Age*, May 20, 1909, 76.

13. Stephen Gray similarly sees "Mind Pictures" as "a definitive example of the Imagist poetry to come." (Gray, *Beatrice Hastings: A Literary Life* [Parklands, South Africa: Penguin Viking, 2004], 243).

A STORY CALLED "MODERNISM"

Tyler Babbie

TYLER BABBIE is a Ph.D. candidate in English at the University of Washington, where he focuses on modernist periodical studies. He is the author of the ongoing blog project Little Review Reviews.

M Y FIRST encounter with Beatrice Hastings was in late November 2012, as I read the November 21, 1912 issue of *The New Age*, downloaded from the Modernist Journals Project. I was in the first day of an ongoing project, a one-century-later immersion in the journals of the MJP. That 1912 issue contained a strange stream-of-consciousness story called "An Affair of Politics." The serendipity of encountering Hastings in the first moments of my immersion became clear later, but at the time I was confused: Who was this author? Had I heard about her, but forgotten? Looking back on that moment, I know the sense of déjà vu was misplaced: I hadn't heard of Hastings before. My confidence in my education led me to believe someone printing experimental stream-of-consciousness short fiction in late 1912 would have been brought to my attention, but I underestimated the vagaries of literary history and the challenges facing women working on experimental forms in the early 20th century.

The intuitive connection that I had with "An Affair of Politics" might have come from my background as a student of modernist poetry. Hastings's experimental works are proto-surrealist, self-consciously working against seamless inter-pretation and readability. Trying to piece together these challenging and compelling stories requires an openness to reading practices we typically associate with poetry and the dense fiction of modernist authors like James Joyce. They also require some knowledge of the cultural moments in which they appear, as they self-consciously engage with their times and make claims for their own value as cutting-edge art relative to other art. They are, like many modernist texts, innovative in form—they are interesting as much for how they create meaning as for what they mean. "An Affair of Politics," for instance, is an enormous paragraph transcribing a flustered upper-class woman's long tirade about the fallout that current events have had on her life: "Well, I said, I could have two boys instead of one of each of the maids and put them to sleep in the harness room the ventilation is perfect but solve the problem I shall it's shameful!"[1] That's just a taste—the story bounds on for many lines, with people shooting guns in the dining room, the family of the house eating the servants' dinners, etc. I suspect that the story is about the upper class' reaction to the implementation of mandatory insurance, a major issue for *The New Age*. Hastings uses modernist techniques to satirize a contemporary issue. Without the claim to permanence implied by fiction published in book form, stories like "An Affair of Politics" explicitly play with the format of the literary magazine, engaging the ability of a magazine to comment, respond, and satirize.[2] While the most formally innovative pieces of Hastings's fiction are usually quite small, perhaps even fragments, they are hugely fascinating for their deft handling of modernist materials in their periodical form. Understanding all this requires context, more context than I had during that first encounter.

Context abounds in the Modernist Journals Project's vast, yet achingly incomplete archive. MJP founder Robert Scholes is a leading expert on Hastings and *The New Age*, so her contributions have always been well-represented there.[3] Sitting down to read a weekly paper as if a subscriber led me to see that Hastings requires a different set of assumptions than reading modernist literature in collections. As the powerful anonymous sub-editor and woman-behind-the-curtain at *The New Age*, Hastings could control her public image. One of the classic features of Hastings at *The New Age* is her ready use of pseudonyms to advance her views, creating them as necessary: even "An Affair of Politics" appeared under the pseudonym Alice Morning, a name she reserved for much of her more-literary work. Others have noted that she was willing to have one pseudonym attack another, feeding the flames of the debates hosted by *The New Age*.[4] Despite this proliferation of pseudonyms, there are frequent nods to the fact that all is not what it seems: in the November 13, 1913 issue R.H.C. (a pseudonym most often used by the editor, A.R. Orage) comments on Hastings's satires of Ezra Pound, writing that "the eclecticism of *The New Age*…is much more apparent than real" and that "every part of *The New Age* hangs together." There is, though, another method to spotting Hastings, even if it is imperfect.

Read *The New Age* in vast quantities while paying attention to the cast of authors, and a certain Hastings-specific style emerges. Though she prided herself on her ability to speak in different voices, her voice remains recognizable behind her many masks, which in itself became a point of pride later—in *The Old "New Age,"* a 1936 pamphlet she wrote to debunk the amount of credit A.R. Orage was taking for *The New Age's* achievements, she encourages readers to locate her by style.[5] Regardless of her retrospective claims, *The New Age* is, for Hastings, news media and artistic medium—the periodical is her political platform and her dramatic stage, and she uses it to push her beliefs while exercising her talents. Everything Hastings wrote for *The New Age* was a diffused performance, a destabilization of the author function that simultaneously exploited the journal's reputation as a space for logical discourse. All of her writings are, in a sense, experimental fiction—even as, admittedly, some experiments fail.

Her long engagement with the journal has an axis that books cannot preserve: that of time. Personae, projects, ideas, narrative arcs, all come and go over the course of Hastings's years at *The New Age*. Hastings's inability to get her work published by reputable presses, repeatedly referenced in *The New Age*, means that until this Unsung Masters volume, it was only accessible in its original, serialized form or in very rare volumes and pamphlets. With the digitization of periodicals online, it is possible to read Hastings casually again. Hastings's texts, her different voices, interwoven with the artistic and philosophical debates of her time, retain their original interrelationships. Hastings needs to be read serially because seriality is a part of her method, as her dramatic experiments with authorial and editorial form pushed through the permeable boundaries of genre.

I hope readers of the short stories in this volume will find them as interesting as I found "An Affair of Politics." The two stories I am about to discuss were published earlier than "An Affair of Politics," and appeared earlier than the beginning of my century-based immersion project: once I got hooked on Hastings, I worked backwards through *The New Age*, hunting for experimental stories because their appearance in such a public sphere and at such early dates has implications for the larger picture of literary modernism, a picture from which Hastings is now conspicuously absent. The first, "Post-Impressionism," is the perfect example of how Hastings's early experimental fictions took part in a larger conversation. "Post-Impressionism" was printed in the January 26, 1911 issue of *The New Age*, where it emerged from the debate surrounding Roger Fry's art exhibition, *Manet and the Post-Impressionists*. This exhibition gave London its first long look at Cezanne, Van Gogh, Matisse, Gauguin, and other continental artists. It kindled a blaze of controversy in both the mainstream papers and in magazines like *The New Age*. The debate over the exhibition hinged on the role of realism in art. Desmond McCarthy, the secretary of the exhibition, writes in the catalogue to the exhibition: "it is the boast of those who believe in this school, that its methods enable the individuality of the artist to find completer self-expression in his work than is possible to those who have committed themselves to representing objects more literally."[6] This secondhand boast on the part of the artists is the kind of claim that would inspire reactions, and ultimately "Post-Impressionism."

The text of "Post-Impressionism" appears in this Unsung Masters volume. It is five short paragraphs separated by asterisks. It is also very strange, and I cannot say I fully understand what it means. Certainly, it is a bold experiment. In January of 1911, most famous modernist works had yet to be published. James Joyce, for one, was wrestling with his publishers over *Dubliners*, and was working on *A Portrait of the Artist as a Young Man*, which is more analogous in style to Hastings's experimental stories. It is not necessary to claim some kind of chronological primacy for Hastings's story, or to delve into the complex scholarship and scholarly politics of the term "modernism." Even so, "Post-Impressionism" appears very early and is tied specifically to the events of late 1910: "In or around December 1910, human character changed," as Virginia Woolf famously quipped in "Mr. Bennett and Mrs. Brown."[7] Woolf, writing in the early 1920's, may have been referencing her friend Roger Fry's exhibition. Returning to the winter of 1910: Hastings was on the scene, as was Arnold Bennett (a renowned author in his time and the titular character in Woolf's "Mr. Bennett and Mrs. Brown.") Both have a role to play in the story of "Post-Impressionism."

The opening, "The Manniquins [sic] wound like a serpent over the grass of the noble domain," fuses poetic rhythm with disorienting imagery, and showcases the weird beauty of Hastings's story. The fact that Hastings still disorients speaks more to the success than the failure of the piece, as it was an attempt to represent reality without being literal. Hastings, who is capable of seemingly effortless eloquence, creates another new voice, and uses it to showcase a different set of capabilities than she does in her journalism, criticism, poetry, or more straightforward fiction. There are many possible reasons for the story's obscurity—it is probably in part a story à clef, written in part for those in the know, in a code we outsiders cannot crack. Some details may have been more legible in the moment of its publication: it is partly set in the Carlton Hotel, which was famously one of the finest and most modern in London. Other mysteries remain.

Some of the difficulties of the story are insoluble, while others can be glossed. In the fourth paragraph, Hastings plays with referential pronouns to create a puzzle, "He wrapped his head in a soft serviette and nursed it on his knee, saying, 'Poor old Baron; do take something to eat, Min.' So Minnie Pinnikin had a plate on the floor at the knee of the head, and he fed her, horribly goggling..." The puzzle of the paragraph, and part of its pleasure, comes from the way the story foregrounds the ambiguity of language. It takes several readings, but the meaning ultimately becomes clear: the unnamed first man is caring for a slightly ill Baron. The first man, who has wrapped the Baron's head in a napkin to alleviate his illness somehow, invites the heroine of the story, Minnie Pinnkin, to eat some food. Minnie then eats while sitting on the floor, presumably on the same level as the Baron, with the first man looming over them, "horribly goggling." It is not a moment with obvious dramatic value—there is not much sustained plot. It is a vivid moment, represented not through the clarity of language, but through its capacity for ambiguity. An ambiguous situation required ambiguous grammar.[8]

The final paragraph in "Post-Impressionism" is even more extreme. I have a hunch that it is a description of purchasing paintings at an artist's flat, which is appropriate enough for a story titled after a recent art exhibition. The man who "hooks" people up from the street does so through his art, by capturing them on canvas. Minnie Pinnikin nearly buys a painting, but her husband stops her. Then, there is a strange encounter with the eyes of the "mock curate," whose goggling eyes recall those of the unnamed man in the prior section. The quick transition between these images produces the surrealist feeling of seeing two images at once—but prior to the emergence of surrealism.

And yet, after all the surrealist fireworks, there is another layer to this story that makes it all the more complex and exciting: in the original, it is printed not as a short story, but as a letter to the editor (and therefore a letter to Orage). Like any letter to the editor, it is marked by its beginning: "Sir,—" a tag that indicates its nature as a letter. It is an intervention in an ongoing debate over the exhibition, and the title "Post-Impressionism" is a topical heading rather than a proper title. Hastings places fiction into the realm of correspondence to take the prestige of the correspondence pages and apply it directly to her story. In *The New Age*, the correspondence pages were a realm for interaction and debate, devoted to rhetoric and logical argument. Hastings was breaking the rules to intervene in a debate, and may have been giving herself the last word. Including the January 26 issue, seven of the prior eight issues of *The New Age* discussed *Manet and the Post-Impressionists* in one way or another, but after the story "Post-Impressionism," the debate falls silent.

The entire course of the debate over *Manet and the Post-Impressionists*, as preserved in *The New Age* is fascinating in its own right, but I will focus on the moments that I believe had the biggest impact on the short story in question. The first key moment is George Calderon's review of the show, which appeared in the November 24, 1910 issue of *The New Age*. Calderon translates the difficult painters from the continent for the culturally savvy but broadly-based readership of *The New Age*, explaining that the value of the paintings comes from a more accurate depiction of reality than realism. In the conclusion of his essay, he urges his readers to go see the various portraits and landscapes of the exhibition, and bids them to "[t]hen go forth and pass along the streets about and note how flat, stale and unprofitable have become all those engravings, pictures and statues in the art dealers' windows, that represent the bare photographic semblance of reality, with dramatic meanings laid on it, not drawn out from it." Calderon's invocation of "bare photography" as the antithesis of art and his insistence that drama is present in reality, not something imposed upon it by an author, were rebukes to the British artistic establishment. That establishment noticed the rebuke and responded vigorously in the correspondence pages of *The New Age*.

Calderon was writing about painting, but another, more regular contributor had taken note of his claims about the exhibition. Arnold Bennett wrote for *The New Age* under the pseudonym Jacob Tonson. He contributed a piece in the December 8, 1910 issue in defense of the exhibition. What makes Bennett's column important for Hastings's story "Post-Impressionism" is the way he presciently saw that there could be an analogy in literature to the works of Cezanne, Matisse, Van Gogh, and the other artists exhibited at the show:

> ...I have permitted myself to suspect that supposing some writer were to come along and do in words what these men have done in paint, I might conceivably be disgusted with nearly the whole of modern fiction, and I might have to begin again. This awkward experience will in all probability not happen, to me, but it might happen to a writer younger than me. At any rate it is a fine thought. The average critic always calls me, both in praise and dispraise, "photographic"; and I always rebut the epithet with disdain, because in the sense meant by the average critic I am not photographic. But supposing that in a deeper sense I were? Supposing a young writer turned up and forced me, and some of

my contemporaries—us who fancy ourselves a bit—to admit that we had been concerning ourselves unduly with [in]essentials,[9] that we had been worrying ourselves to achieve infantile realisms? Well that day, would be a great and a disturbing day—for us. And we should see what we should see.[10]

This is the moment when Bennett confronts the unpleasant fact that his cutting-edge literary realism may have encountered something that will surpass it. He indicates photography in a double move, rejecting that his art is photographic, while admitting that it may have elements of photography. While it is hard to say exactly what Bennett means by "a deeper sense" of photography, I think contrasting his style with that of the Hastings story might illustrate what he meant. I believe that Hastings's story was a direct answer to Bennett's implied challenge to "some young writer."

"Modernism" is now a word so encrusted with meanings that it is difficult to define, but it was less common during the 1910's. Hastings may have picked up the term from R.A. Scott-James, who used modernism as a term to describe literature in *Romance and Modernism*, a book of literary criticism, which was reviewed in *The New Age* on October 10, 1911.[11] Hastings may have had Scott-James's definition of modernism in mind when she titled her short story. Modernism was available to her as a literary term, but it would have been very new. Her story is one of the earlier uses of "modernism" in reference to literature in the Modernist Journals Project. It may be the first published work in English that self-designates as "modernism."

"Modernism" takes place in the same fictional universe as "Post-Impressionism," as it contains the recurring character Valerie, sometimes identified as Katherine Mansfield *à clef*.[12] Like "Post-Impressionism," "Modernism" bounces the reader from scene to scene without clear transitions. Even though it is very brief, careful reading reveals that there are three main actions: the first, exploring London with a man identified only as the French Jew, the second, examining Valerie's new clothes, and the third, a vacation trip to Brighton.

Again, the opening is significant: "It is very like life to find all the swell restaurants in Capetown crowded." "It is very like life," which in the story is a rueful aside, contains a side-comment on realism in its half-concealed invocation of "lifelike." Readers might expect the story to take place in Capetown, perhaps expecting it due to the author's background, but the restaurants listed were all famous establishments on the Strand in London. Hastings overlays South Africa onto London, disrupting the geography of the capital by invoking the colony. This is the first of many moments that may have been clearer to the audience of the story than to me. There is a chance, though, that this was a slip at some point in production: South Africa does not figure elsewhere in the story, so it is possible that "in" was added to "Capetown crowded," which was supposed to be descriptive of how hot and crowded the restaurants were. Driven to seek shelter from the sweltering heat, the narrator and her unnamed companion, a French Jew, search among the fashionable restaurants for one with an electric fan. The French Jew, overcome with emotion at seeing the opera hall where Jenny Lind sang, gives a slight hint to chronology—Lind retired from singing in 1883.[13] Then, the abrupt transition to Valerie's wardrobe, gathered from dress agencies, which were high-end consignment shops. Then another abrupt transition, to the sea.

They go to meet a friend named Polly by the sea, and incidentally, run into an Oxford poet as well. My favorite moment in the story is when the narrator explains their confusion on learning that "sloughed" and "slowed" are homophones. At first, the narrator does not want to accept the difference between her expectations and reality, but sums up her acceptance with the response: "but there was the mud," an illustration of the narrator's preconceptions about language, absorbed via reading, encountering intransigent reality.

As with "Post-Impressionism," "Modernism" is a product of its context. Hastings writes anonymous criticism under the heading "Present-Day Criticism," or so she claims in *The Old "New Age."* The January 18th, 1912 issue's "Present-Day Criticism" is a manifesto on contemporary fiction and its failings. Echoing Arnold Bennett's anxieties of 1910, Hastings's persona of "Present-Day Criticism" finds realist novels unsatisfactory. In this column, she attacks the leading novelists of the time, first, the original Scott-James modernist, Thomas Hardy: "In Mr. Hardy's 'Jude the Obscure' we are shown not characters but the whimsies of two persons... They are not people at all, but a congeries of moods. The action seems to be invented from day to day in order to exhibit some fresh mood." Joseph Conrad, H.G. Wells, and finally, Arnold Bennett, Jacob Tonson himself, receive corrosive correctives. Here's Bennett's: "The latest addition to the gallery of inconsequents, 'Hilda Lessways,' is also the most tiresome. This figure has no more character than a badly-fixed weather-vane."[14] In summary, these characters "are untrue to human nature, and unworthy of any man's pen. To set them out as realistic representations of men and women is simply silly. The world would be one Bedlam if these morbid egotists were representative." Here is the climax of the essay:

> We need now in realist fiction men with psychic knowledge, in whom truth is settled, with whom truth is the ruling passion, upon whom everything that is untrue palls. If they deal with untruth, their treatment of it will detect it, and untruth detected is dead from that moment, though its glamour persist still awhile. Such realists as these may write nothing but romances; they will not, in any case, describe furniture like tradesmen, scenery like drunkards, moral and mental changelings like quacks, and toss us that for Realism.

Realism, then, is still the goal, but not a realism of externals. Authentic realism is truth, not description, and especially truth in characterization. This essay's strength is not necessarily its depth, as the conclusions that it comes to are relatively superficial until placed next to the other text that references contemporary literature in this issue of *The New Age*: "Modernism." Both "Post-Impressionism" and "Modernism" exist in dialogue with and alongside criticism. In these two moments, Hastings's experimental mode is a kind of criticism by example, first in answering Bennett's challenge, second by illustrating her own critical beliefs in the essay quoted above.

To work backward for a moment: this iteration of "Present-Day Criticism" opened with an argument about art in general: "There are not many moods of Art. Admiration is one, hope is one, satire is one, humour is one; and, whenever a passion rules, there is a mood of art. Love is not one. Love is a phase of temperament, more or less ephemeral-it has no relation to truth." In the context of the search for a new, more potent realism encouraged by the rest of the essay, this introduction delineates the modes of literary truth. Love stories are out, but passion is in. Satire and humor are then placed next to admiration and hope as modes in which passion and truth are possible, more possible than in realism. It implies that satire is more realist than descriptive realism. This is a key to understanding Beatrice Hastings's works of experimental fiction: they are, on some level, satires. Combined with the conclusion from above, then, a satire with realistic characters would be adequate to the needs of contemporary literature, while melodramatic descriptive realism is not.

"Modernism," then, is the new realism called for by "Present-Day Criticism," but it makes clear that the shift will take more than a refinement of the prior genre. Hastings replaces the furniture, scenery, and romance of realism with attention to form and prose that focuses on detail. She replaces exhibitions of unbalanced protagonists with subtle conversational cues that let readers divine the nature of the protagonist for themselves. Instead of flowing informational text, Hastings makes the reader piece together the details of the story: it will remain opaque without proper attention to spoken language, in parallel to its nature as written language. Hastings includes a lengthy discussion of the relationship of speech to written literature in *The Old "New Age,"* including this insult that she ultimately turns into a compliment: "I was once called by a certain person who shall be nameless 'a speaker disguised as a writer.'"[15]

This handful of stories show that Hastings was a modernist pioneer, but it remains a handful. There are hints, though, that the stories are fragments of a larger project, a lost novel that might have done more to establish Hastings's reputation. In *Modigliani and the Artists of Montparnasse*, Kenneth Wayne included selections from a French manuscript of a novel by Hastings titled *Minnie Pinnikin*, found by chance in the Museum of Modern Art in New York.[16] *Modigliani and the Artists of Montparnasse* includes three translated chapters from the novel, describing it in the introduction as a "long-lost novella about her relationship with Amadeo Modigliani during the years 1914 to 1916, presumably written during these same years." This does not, however, make perfect sense chronologically. The English language experimental stories were published between 1910 and 1914, but apparently Hastings met Modigliani in 1914. This is when he begins to appear in her articles in *The New Age*. The stories, then, are not just surrealist reflections of Modigliani, but were probably revised to incorporate details from her life with him. Wayne's introduction notes that the manuscript in the MoMA is in French, but speculates that there was an original, now-lost English version based on a note that the French draft was a translation. The prior stories published in *The New Age* support this conclusion. Details from the story "Post-Impressionism" reappear in the MoMA manuscript, including a description of "fishing men from the street, swinging them with his long hands," imagery taken from "Post-Impressionism." The story precedes the artistic movement that supposedly shaped it. I wonder if Hastings influenced Modigliani's modernism, rather than the other way around.

Calling Hastings a modernist experimental writer adds yet another identity to the voluble, paradoxical, and contradictory crowd of her personae. There is an individual, historical human behind them all, but it seems impossible to approach that person through the crowd. These stories are difficult to the point of opacity, but their very opacity is revelatory, because they admit forthrightly that they will not be solved, unlike the other personae who often encourage complicity. Even recurring voices change over time, and projects come and go, as Hastings's interests shifted between genres, producing poems, translations, essays, philosophy, and cultural commentary in turn. Within this vast corpus, the handful of experimental stories push the self-creating and self-differentiating project farthest, harnessing Hastings's talent for creating new voices to the work of reinventing fiction from its roots. And yet, claims like these call out for caveats and careful distinctions, especially since the argument rests on a handful of stories, which may be fragments themselves. Sweeping claims fall apart during microanalyses of modernism because modernisms are particular and change quickly in time. The stories themselves reflect this as they whip through time and space without transition. "Very surprising, the strength of his thin white hands," as the narrator describes the artist in "Post-Impressionism." The stories, small as they are, have their own surprising strength, founded not in their intelligibility, but in that capacity to surprise.

NOTES

1. Alice Morning (Beatrice Hastings), "An Affair of Politics," *The New Age*, November 21, 1912, 67-68.

2. Carey Snyder, "Katherine Mansfield and the *New Age* School of Satire," *The Journal of Modern Periodical Studies* 1:2 (2010): 125-158. Snyder writes

about Hastings's literary relationship with Katherine Mansfield, showing how Hastings's satirical bent helped Mansfield develop as a modernist author.

3. Robert Scholes, *Paradoxy of Modernism* (New Haven: Yale University Press, 2006).

4. John Carswell discusses an example of Hastings using pseudonyms to attack herself in *Lives and Letters: A.R. Orage, Beatrice Hastings, Katherine Mansfield, John Middleton Murry, S.S. Koteliansky, 1906-1957* (London: Faber and Faber, 1978), 59-60.

5. Beatrice Hastings, *The Old "New Age": Orage and Others* (London: Blue Moon Press, 1936). See "Finding the Man in the Style," 38-42.

6. Desmond MacCarthy, "The Post-Impressionists," *Manet and the Post-Impressionists* (London: Ballantyne, 1911), 7.

7. Virginia Woolf, "Mr. Bennett and Mrs. Brown," (London, The Hogarth Press, 1924). Readers may notice that Woolf's thesis is largely the same as Hastings's.

8. Aspects of this story may have a twin in a story by Katherine Mansfield. Mansfield's story, "Germans at Meat," is similarly about English people eating with Germans. Several critics have made a convincing claim for Mansfield's importance as a modernist innovator, most of whom acknowledge Hastings's influence (or at least her proximity) to Mansfield. They share an experimental edge, though Hastings carries it much farther into the realm of the surreal and the opaque than Mansfield. This is not to diminish Mansfield—I think both authors gained from their willingness to experiment with new kinds of writing.

9. The original printing of the essay had misprinted "essentials" for "inessentials" here, which was clarified in the subsequent issue of *The New Age*.

10. John Carswell cites this same passage, implying that the unnamed young author would be Virginia Woolf—an anachronism, but it is telling that he reaches for it.

11. "Modernism and Romance," *The New Age*, October 10, 1908, 47.

12. Stephen Gray disputes the identification of Valerie as Mansfield in his biography of Hastings: *Beatrice Hastings: A Literary Life* (London: Viking, 2004), 251.

13. Curiously, the man is identified as a French-speaking Jew, which immediately calls to mind Hasting's lover Amedeo Modigliani, but the biographical record claims that Modigliani and Hastings did not meet until 1914.

14. Beatrice Hastings, "Present-Day Criticism," *The New Age*, January 18, 1912, 277.

15. *The Old "New Age,"* 40.

16. Kenneth Wayne, *Modigliani and the Artists of Montparnasse* (Buffalo: Harry N. Abrams Inc., 2002) 204-211.

THE LOST BACCHANTE: BEATRICE HASTINGS AND THE WAR YEARS

Celia Kingsbury

CELIA KINGSBURY is a professor at the University of Central Missouri. She is the author of For Home and Country: World War I Propaganda on the Home Front *(University of Nebraska Press, 2010) and* The Peculiar Sanity of War: Hysteria in the Literature of World War I *(Texas Tech University Press, 2002). Her work on modernism and the First World War has also appeared in* Modern Fiction Studies *and* Conradiana.

PUBLISHED in the June 9, 1910 issue of *The New Age*, "The Lost Bacchante," undoubtedly Beatrice Hastings's most famous poem, declares in the voice of one of Bacchus's acolytes, "I'll bind up my ruddy hair / In a band of tendrils plucked from the vine, / And ivy and grapes I will wear."[1] Prophetic down to the last grape, the poem describes Hastings four years later as she negotiated the bohemian streets of World War I Paris. By the fall of 1914, with the German army threatening to invade Paris, Hastings and her new-found lover Amedeo Modigliani attended a fancy dress ball to benefit the artist's canteen which kept many penniless artists, Modigliani included, alive during the war.

Broke and unable to afford costumes, Modigliani ripped one of Hastings's silk dresses to make it more revealing and then painted the dress, along with parts of Beatrice, with flowers and vines. Living bacchante and walking Modigliani, Hastings showed up barefoot at the event, artist in tow. Her triumph was short-lived. Jealous of the attention Beatrice received, and characteristically drunk, Modigliani ejected her, as Stephen Gray claims, high on "either hashish or whiskey, but at any rate blotto," from the party. Beatrice remained in the dress in the wet streets of Paris allegedly running from Modigliani for days. The truth of this story, as with much of Beatrice Hastings's life, is open for debate, at least in its details. According to Gray, this story and others, including one of Hastings dressed as Madame de Pompadour and carrying a basket of ducklings, "have ensured that she never be taken seriously and have damaged her reputation. They also reek of woman-hatred."[2] Misogyny aside, one of Modigliani's most famous paintings is of Beatrice as Madame de Pompadour, mistress of Louis XV, eighteenth century French monarch.[3] Hastings's willingness to serve as the artist's sitter, as well as his canvas, reflects a larger commitment to a Modernist agenda and an avant-garde life. Hastings's life with Modigliani, while it occupied over two years of the war, was only a small part of a self-creation that became transgressive, a strong feminist statement made well before such statements were appreciated, even among the avant-garde. From her many pseudonyms, of which Beatrice Hastings was only one, to her claims that she gave birth to and lost a child, Hastings created a life that was itself art; she was indeed a performance artist in the service of the new and the radical, but most of all, in the service of her writing.

Hastings's war writings began before the war in her association with *The New Age* and A.R. Orage. Orage and Hastings met at a Theosophical Society lecture, another debatable fact according to John Carswell, although both were followers of Theosophist writer and alleged clairvoyant Madam Blavatsky.[4] What is not debatable is that Orage and Hastings began a relationship that continued in and out of the press until her death in 1943. Before she became Alice Morning who produced "Impressions de Paris" for *The New Age*, Hastings published poetry as well as incidental pieces under various pseudonyms. In April of 1914, she went to Paris to begin her "Impressions" and her life as Alice Morning, reporting on Paris as a tourist might until the start of the war. Following an entry called "The Plum Tree" on April 30, Alice Morning's "Impressions" begin on May 21, 1914, almost a month before the assassination of Austrian Archduke Franz Josef Ferdinand, an event which initially didn't provoke much interest in Europe or England. The tone of the first entry is flippant, almost schoolgirlish, certainly not that of the cynical woman Hastings would become by the end of the war. Alluding to her departure from Victoria station, Alice begins, "When the train had fairly moved, I regretted not to have kissed the dear…,"[5] a reference not to Orage, but to Wyndham Lewis, who saw her off, getting her safely out of Orage's hair.[6] The rest of the entry is what can only be called prattle. Alice rambles on about teaching her future children, something Hastings had declared she would never have, about "the new movements in art," about having encounters with rude English and rude French who don't like her accent, and finally, about really not wanting to see the tourist sights.[7]

Over the summer of 1914, Alice/Beatrice set up housekeeping in Montparnasse, worked on her French, and, as did everyone else, basically ignored any notion that war was in the works. During this period, the gap between the tone of Alice's "Impressions" and the reality of Beatrice's life widened. By her June 4 entry, she writes of a sculptor in "cap, scarf, and corduroy" whom she refers to as a "pale and ravishing villain."[8] At the time, Modigliani was in fact sculpting, and continued to do so until Beatrice convinced him he was a better painter. Modigliani was not the only avant-garde personality to cross paths with Hastings. Picasso was in Paris at the time, as well as Guillaume Apollinaire, who was later wounded in the war. Gertrude Stein was there living with her brother, although there is no indication that Hastings had any connections with her. Max Jacob was a close associate and shared her house when she moved to Montmartre. And yet this life of hers for the most part stayed out of the pages of *The New Age*. Only later, when she began an open feud with Orage, did she conduct her life in print.

By July 2, some of the glib quality of "Impressions" has worn off, but not enough to suit Orage, who is not happy with Alice Morning. Alice has been criticized for not going "Baedekking." After rejecting what she refers to as the custom-house view of cities, Alice muses that "[s]ometimes I think I can see in my face an impression of all the steps I've mounted to inspect marvels."[9] At the top of one those staircases, Alice views the work of Picasso and Rousseau, neither of which she likes. The rest of the piece is devoted to the kind of snobbery that favors bad art over masterpieces and gossips ruthlessly. Later going on again about Rousseau, Hastings names Modigliani, who has called Rousseau's work "trés joli." Still sculpting at this point, Modigliani has left one of his stone heads in Alice's studio. In an observation which might make a twenty-first century art lover shudder with envy, Alice tells readers, "One of Modigliani's stone heads was on a table below the painting of Picasso, and the contrast between the true thing and the true-to-life thing nearly split me." Alice wants to offer to buy the stone head, but doesn't ask because Modigliani was forever giving away or selling for nothing his work, a habit Alice takes to task, as well as his habit of bathing every two hours in the garden of his studio.[10] Although she names Modigliani here, she maintains a discrete journalistic distance. In these early Alice Morning pieces, Hastings begins to develop the philosophical voice that allowed her to keep her "Impressions" going until she became tired of the war and all its destruction. During this period, around Bastille Day 1914, Beatrice went back to London. As Alice explains in her next "Impression," "I went to England last Tuesday. Someone wrote me that some women were up to something, so I had to go see what it was. Rien de tout, believe me! I never knew anything that had so little in it."[11] As she was leaving Paris, however, Modigliani made a terrible row, following her to the station where she had to insult his sculpting to get him to desist. Once again, private becomes public, but Alice is still discreet keeping the reality of her escapades under wraps. In the first few months of 1914, right before the defining moment of the twentieth century literally exploded in her face, Hastings is breaking off with one lover to return to another, and herein lies the misogyny Gray alludes to. Modigliani had little flack over his multiple affairs or his drinking and drug use, while Hastings did. Even André Salmon, who as Gray argues, saw Beatrice as Modigliani's muse just as an earlier Beatrice was to Dante, notes her fondness for whiskey when she lived in Montparnasse. According to Salmon, Hastings was often so drunk, she believed the rat that plagued her in her studio glowed in the dark.[12]

What the transgressive Beatrice found in London at *The New Age* besides Orage was, among others, Ezra Pound, characteristically snarky about Modigliani, and on the verge of entering his Fascist period. *The New Age* had been a Socialist journal, funded partly by George Bernard Shaw, but Gray maintains it was about to turn decidedly right.[13] Pound had assumed Beatrice's editorial position, but she and Modigliani needed her reasonably regular paycheck for her "Impressions de Paris." Hastings basically settled her affairs with former lover Orage and went back to Modigliani and to Paris on the eve of war.

Alice Morning's last "Impression" before the start of the war is one paragraph—Gray claims Orage cut it to that length without her permission.[14] By way of opening, Alice declares "It is all over. I'm finished. I've been to the Louvre." This "Baedekking," and the affordability of it, have her in a dither and she vows to write no more impressions.[15] Cut or not, the levity, and perhaps irony, of the piece occurring two days before the war began in

France dissipates in the entries that follow. On August 13, she is trying to get a permit to remain in France and, at the same time, buying plums to make jam, which she can't do because there is no sugar to be had. Jam, she says, would be as good as meat for her purposes. She makes an inventory of her food supplies—sardines, "bad rice," and sixteen eggs.[16] These early "Impressions" fail to invoke Hasting's later anti-war feelings, but instead record a first-hand account of Paris under the threat of a German invasion. News is scarce and often unreliable. Scaremongers incur the full force of her wrath. The British Consul wants three francs fifty for her permit papers, and she refuses to pay until her lack of them becomes too much of a threat to anyone walking the streets with her and she finally gives up. She eats endless sardines and goes out in spite of German bombs falling. Wounded soldiers begin showing up and draw crowds who want to feed them. She gets on the wrong tram and winds up in Montmartre, newly full of skyscrapers, where she enters the "loath-some-looking" Church of the Sacred Heart. Here she lunches with an "anti-militarist" friend she runs into; lunch is a "wonderful, eatable beef-steak" and French table wine which she despises. In a rare moment when Alice's night life intrudes itself into the pages of *The New Age*, she declares that instead of the wine, she "would feel safer tipping off a glass of whiskey neat..."[17] Prior to this jaunt, she tells readers that the sale of absinthe has been halted, and she explains that, "the result is a rush for much viler potions."[18]

Two issues dominate the early war "Impressions." The first is her absolute sympathy for soldiers, especially wounded soldiers, for families desperate to get word from their soldiers, and for the stoicism of families who have lost soldiers already. Less than three weeks into the war, she writes in admiration of a Frenchwoman who has already lost two sons, but still "spoke for ten minutes with the concierge and never referred to the loss."[19] During this period, however, Alice's pet peeve is with English suffragettes, with whom Hastings had previously crossed paths, or pens. Still ambivalent in her "Impressions" about votes for women, Alice mocks British feminist Christabel Pankhurst, who had come out wholeheartedly in favor of the war. Latching on to the phrase "to do what good I can elsewhere," Alice calls the movement's response "a revolting amusement," then declares that she "wouldn't give [her] femme de chambre's nail-parings for the theatrical spirit of all the suffragettes [she had] ever met."[20] While she never names her femme de chambre, Alice maintains a strong relationship with her and tries to keep her employed to the extent she can. The feminist issue, on the other hand, frequently riles Alice, who nevertheless lives the life of a free and unencumbered woman, the often abusive, often clinging Modigliani, notwithstanding. Commenting on her newfound tendency to strike up conversations with "the wildest kind of acquaintance," Alice describes a meeting with "a most preposterous cocotte" who hoped to use the war as a way to make a new life by marrying an English soldier. One of Alice's "friends" has suggested that she stop wasting her time writing for *The New Age* and write a novel about "the dangerous age" instead. Alice has talked about the novel before, but insists that "there isn't enough matter in it to satisfy a really self-respecting novel." What follows this remark is a curious statement on marriage and female longing, the potential plot of her novel. Female dissatisfaction seems to grow out of married life, and, she suggests, "women past their youth who imagine that they crave merely an orgy, really covet adoration...."[21] While Alice is out looking for war news, her femme de chambre spills a lamp full of paraffin all over the above remarks and has hung them out to dry in the scullery. "Reader," Alice muses, "you nearly never knew about my chat with the naughty lady." Still on the Pankhursts, Hastings notes that she has had complaints from some of her readers about her "neglect of the Great" and about noticing that, for instance, on the day of mobilization, the French prostitutes were out in the streets, modestly dressed, but still wearing vivid make-up. The upshot of this tirade is that the ladies of the night are better guardians of civilization than "the absurd Christabel."[22]

By early October, the period of the fancy dress ball, Alice is very nearly starving. The mail is not coming through and thus her check from *The New Age* is delayed. Still a bit ignorant of French culture, she has been in a butcher shop and bought, thinking it was steak, "*cheval*," which she can't bear to write out in English. Her femme de chambre tells her to look at the sign above the shop before she buys next time. But the circumstances are too dire to dispose of the horse meat, and Alice feels "quite disgraced" having eaten it. Before the long awaited check arrives, Alice is surviving on milk and bread, and in fact going for days without eating. The only food on her shelf is a tin of peas, which she cannot abide. In this lengthy "Impression," now "of Paris," not "de Paris," Alice still argues the plight of starving artists and lambasts the bourgeoisie for continuing to eat and drink unscathed without sharing. Out in the street because she is bored in her studio, her "coat becomes heavy, [her] weakest eye hurts, and the wind cracks the skin on [her] face."[23]

Hastings's biographer Stephen Gray is vague, perhaps deliberately, about the exact date of the fancy dress ball for which Beatrice is painted as a Bacchae. Nevertheless, in this same hunger-stricken "Impression," complaining of the sudden cold in Paris, Alice has explained that "last Tuesday I wore a tussore frock without a coat."[24] Undoubtedly, this is the tussore frock Modigliani would destroyed in the name of art. Additionally, during this period of cold and hunger, her concierge has come in to tell her a friend has dropped by to invite her to dinner on the following Wednesday. "Empty news!" Alice declares. "[She] will be dead before then." Wishing no longer for food but champagne, Alice thinks that if she lives long enough for the dinner, she will enjoy the company. Later her friend arrives to explain that the dinner is "an economic concern arranged by some artists," most certainly the fancy dress ball. By the end of the paragraph, Alice has been to the dinner and reports on the nationalities there, including Spaniard and Italian—Picasso and Modigliani.[25] If this is indeed the event about which all of Montparnasse and half of Paris talked, readers of *The New Age* never knew it.

Among Hasting's English friends from *The New Age*, Katherine Mansfield may be the most notable. Ten years younger than Hastings, Mansfield found a fellow traveler in Hastings, who began publishing Mansfield's stories in *The New Age*. When the two met, Mansfield had just broken off a short-lived marriage to tenor George Bowden, possibly because, according to John Carswell, she might have thought she was pregnant by another man. The marriage to Bowden was disastrous and the alleged pregnancy might have occurred after Mansfield married Bowden when Mansfield went to Liverpool to join Garnet Trowell, by whom she may have thought she was pregnant to begin with. Carswell deduces that the pregnancy might have been phantom, or that she miscarried in Bavaria where she had been dispatched by her mother who came in from New Zealand to stave off further damage to Katherine's reputation.[26] Hastings, who, writing as Beatrice Tina, had claimed to have had and lost a child,[27] forms a special, if short-lived, bond with Mansfield.

Gray records several Mansfield trips to Paris during 1915 when Hastings was living in the house in Montmartre. It is difficult to detach the details of these visits from the gossip-column tone Gray adopts in his summary of the decaying relationship between the two women who may well have been lovers themselves at one point.[28] Nevertheless, Mansfield seems to have been momentarily off John Middleton Murry and in Paris to bring news from Orage and to pursue a relationship with writer Francis Carco, who, to Mansfield's chagrin, had gone off to war. Mansfield was, without doubt, a dedicated writer. At the same time, she was as openly frank about her relationships with men as was Hastings. But ultimately Mansfield disapproved of Hastings's behavior because of her drinking and the violent nature of Hastings's relationship with

Modigliani. In a letter to Murry, with whom she is corresponding, if not "with," Mansfield declares, "[S]he is ruined. There is no doubt of it—I love her, but I take an intense, cold interest in noting the signs." The signs are Beatrice telling Mansfield about being drunk on various occasions and then saying, "Of course the people here simply love me for it. There hasn't been a woman of feeling here—since the war—but now I am going to be careful."[29] Mansfield claims to be "off drink" and tells Murry that the last time she was drunk, she was with Beatrice. At the end of this observation she says in French that she will never return, but return she does, sharing a Zeppelin raid. Murry writes back that "B. just hadn't enough to pull her through."[30] Hastings also shows up in Mansfield's biography, where she is treated rudely. Biographer Anthony Alpers discusses the same supposed pregnancy incident and quotes L.M. (Ida Baker), who was "'sure that Beatrice Hastings had been in some way responsible.'"[31] Among the facts Alpers reports concerning the incident is that after it was over, Mansfield and Hastings were at the beach together.[32]

The tabloid nature of both lives speaks once again to the idea that Beatrice Hastings, at least, was an evolving self-creation. A transgressive woman during a time of female transgression, Hastings was in some ways not exceptional, and, if perhaps she had written that novel, she might have been remembered as well as some of her contemporaries, including Mansfield. During the nearly two years she spent as Modigliani's mistress, the pair engaged in legendary rows, one in which Beatrice was hurled through a window into the garden of her Montmartre home,[33] and later incidents in the same garden allegedly involving guns. Gray, citing several sources, addresses Beatrice's behavior while at the same time questioning the accuracy of those sources, including Charles Beadle, who claimed to know Beatrice and Modigliani, but refers to Modigliani as Modi, not Dedo, which his friends called him.[34] Yet certain "truths" emerge in the often turbulent life of Hastings. She spoke her mind and was not afraid to engage in behavior that flaunted middle-class morality. She endured hunger and cold to remain in Paris while a war raged only miles away. If she drank excessively, so did many of her contemporaries.

The last of Alice Morning's "Impressions," what Gray calls an "allegory of her life in Paris at war,"[35] appears on November 25, 1915. In it, as Gray notes, Hastings relates an anecdote involving some cows being taken to the slaughterhouse. One of the cows breaks loose and runs wild through the streets until she is captured and led to her fate. Whether or not the stray cow is meant to represent Beatrice herself, Gray notwithstanding, must be up for debate. Written as a newspaper tidbit, the piece names the farmer and others involved in the chase and never uses first person pronouns, which all of the previous "Impressions" do.[36] If not an allegory of Hastings's life, the piece serves as a sort of nose thumbing at Orage, as does the "Baedekking" piece that ushered in the war. Alice Morning appears again in *The New Age* as the author of "Feminine Fables" and other assorted fictions, as well as articles on French pronunciation. Then in July of 1916, she begins her "Peace Notes," strongly worded arguments against the war. Orage published these sundry articles even though many of them included public debates with him.

While art lovers may view Modigliani's portraits of Beatrice without realizing who she is, she may certainly be touted as an unsung master. Her "Impressions of Paris" stand as a record of life, one part of life at least, during the cataclysm of the First World War. Her personal life perhaps stands as another. Modernist fiction produced many larger-than-life heroines, from Mrs. Dalloway to Brett Ashley and Sylvia Tietjens, to the darker portrayals of Nora Flood and Robin Vote of Djuna Barnes's *Nightwood*. In the process of reconstructing the Montmartre Hastings lived in in 1915, Stephen Gray alludes to a little-known silent film series called *Les Vampires*[37] also filmed in 1915 in a Paris curiously devoid of war paraphernalia. Having seen this serial, I find Gray's explanation of it only partially accurate. According to

Gray, the crime syndicate, Les Vampires, depicted in the films, represented a real life threat to law and order that existed during the war. But the most compelling part of the serial which Gray only alludes to is the French actress Musidora, who also plays a villain in the serial *Judex* about a wronged and vengeance-seeking family. In *Les Vampires*, Musidora is a criminal and a thief who often wears a catsuit to commit her crimes. The most interesting part of Musidora's portrayal of Irma Vep in the serial is her relationships to the men, one of whom she marries. Depicted at parties, Musidora dances and imbibes wantonly and seductively. A wonderful villain, she is clearly transgressive, almost masculine, in her behavior, her curves in the catsuit notwithstanding.[38]

If Beatrice Hastings's behavior did indeed keep her from becoming more notable in the world of literary modernism, Gray's accusation of misogyny may be accurate. Still, she performed her art with vigor and a certain amount of grace. The character Hastings created during the war, not only Alice Morning but herself at that moment, performed war-time bohemian Paris to the fullest of her abilities. After writing about her so-called lack of a position on the war in a lengthy entry of "Impressions of Paris" dated July 22, 1915, Hastings describes reading what she refers to as a "fashionable novel" about a genius female pianist who is brought down by her own bad behavior by the end of the book. Referring to the book as "thoroughly lowering," Hastings goes on to say, "[i]t would be a sign of some beginnings of feminine culture if similarly spiteful novels were generally ostracized" instead of being taken on vacation as reading material. More perhaps than the escaped cow from the last Alice Morning entry in *The New Age*, the degraded pianist serves as an example of talented transgressive women everywhere and certainly as a metaphor in this "Impression" for the often pilloried Hastings herself. Rambling as Alice Morning sometimes did, she continues by citing an allusion to her "Impressions" in *Athenaeum* which calls her "outspoken," and goes on to say that she "wastes much of her superfluous...energy on New Age by-paths." The most obvious of those by-paths, although not a *New Age* one, is her life as performance artist. Devoted bacchante, insistent on equal sexual freedom, Hastings paid the price of the degraded pianist in that bad potboiler by being chastised in the little magazines of Modernism. She concludes the above "Impression" with the observation that "one doesn't write Impressions with an eye on Immortality."[39] Perhaps not. But in that feminine culture she imagines, she should have remained closer to immortal than she might have supposed.

NOTES

1. Beatrice Hastings, "Three Poems," *The New Age*, June 9, 1910, 124.

2. Stephen Gray, *Beatrice Hastings: A Literary Life* (Johannesburg: Penguin Books, 2004), 311-314. Gray cites André Salmon as his source for the details of the painted dress.

3. A great intellect, as was Hastings, Madame de Pompadour was a fashion icon, who, among other things, leant her name to a men's hairstyle, popular in the 1950's among rock and rollers, such as Elvis Presley. In the 21st century, Madame de Pompadour appears in an episode of *Dr. Who*, in which Matt Smith's Doctor appears to be quite smitten with her.

4. John Carswell, *Lives and Letters: A.R. Orage, Katherine Mansfield, Beatrice Hastings, John Middleton Murray, and S.S Koteliansky, 1906-1957* (New York: New Directions, 1978), 30.

5. Alice Morning (Beatrice Hastings), "Impressions of Paris," *The New Age*, May 21, 1914, 68.

6. John Carswell, *Lives and Letters*, 90.

7. Morning (Beatrice Hastings), ibid.

8. Morning (Beatrice Hastings), "Impressions," *The New Age*, June 4, 1914, 115.

9. Morning (Beatrice Hastings), "Impressions," *The New Age*, July 2, 1914, 210.

10. Morning (Beatrice Hastings), "Impressions," *The New Age*, July 9, 1914, 235-36.

11. Morning (Beatrice Hastings), "Impressions," *The New Age*, July 16, 1914, 259.

12. Stephen Gray, *Beatrice Hastings: A Literary Life*, 285. Later, Katherine Mansfield also takes Hastings to task for drinking too much, to the extent that she threatens to end their friendship.

13. Ibid., 287-88.

14. Ibid., 288.

15. Morning (Beatrice Hastings), "Impressions," *The New Age*, July 30, 1914, 307.

16. Morning (Beatrice Hastings), "Impressions," *The New Age*, August 13, 1914, 350.

17. Morning (Beatrice Hastings), "Impressions," *The New Age*, September 24, 1914, 501.

18. Morning (Beatrice Hastings), "Impressions," *The New Age*, August 27, 1914, 394.

19. Morning (Beatrice Hastings), "Impressions," *The New Age*, August 20, 1914, 371.

20. Morning (Beatrice Hastings), "Impressions," *The New Age*, September 24, 1914, 501.

21. Ibid., 502.

22. Ibid.

23. Morning (Beatrice Hastings), "Impressions," *The New Age*, October 8, 1914, 549-51.

24. Ibid., 550.

25. Ibid., 551.

26. John Carswell, *Lives and Letters*, 56-57.

27. Beatrice Tina (Beatrice Hastings), *Woman's Worst Enemy: Woman* (London: The New Age Press, 1909), 1-4. Tina/Hastings declares, "I bear the stigma on my soul of an unwilling maternity...The pain and degradation [of which] destroyed for ever [sic] that barrier of golden illusion which had always stood between my soul and the vulgar horrors of human existence" (3).

28. Stephen Gray, *Beatrice Hastings: A Literary Life*, 336.

29. Ibid., 333.

30. Ibid., 336.

31. Antony Alpers, *The Life of Katherine Mansfield* (New York: Penguin Books, 1982), 123.

32. Ibid., 124.

33. Stephen Gray, *Beatrice Hastings: A Literary Life*, 344-45.

34. Ibid., 369.

35. Ibid., 350-52.

36. Morning (Beatrice Hastings), "Impressions," *The New Age*, November 25, 1915, 84.

37. Stephen Gray, *Beatrice Hastings: A Literary Life*, 348.

38. *Les Vampires.* writ. and dir. Louis Feuillade. 417 min., Gaumont, 1996. DVD. Restored by The Cinémathèque Française, the 2-disc set comes in a slipcase decorated with a drawing of Musidora in her catsuit and high-heeled boots, lounging languidly in a chair.

39. Morning (Beatrice Hastings), "Impressions," *The New Age*, July 22, 1915, 276-77.

EDITORS' NOTES
& ACKNOWLEDGEMENTS

EDITORS' NOTES

BENJAMIN JOHNSON is an associate professor at the University of Central Missouri. His articles on modern poetry and culture have appeared in venues including *Texas Studies in Literature and Language, Arizona Quarterly,* and *The Wallace Stevens Journal.*

ERIKA JO BROWN is a Ph.D. student in literature and creative writing at the University of Houston. She holds an M.F.A. from the Iowa Writers' Workshop and a B.A. from Cornell University. She is the author of the poetry collection *I'm Your Huckleberry* (Brooklyn Arts Press) and currently serves as a poetry editor for *Gulf Coast.*

ACKNOWLEDGEMENTS

The editors wish to thank Joan Sutcliffe for her archival support at the H.P.B. Library of the Canadian Theosophical Association; Unsung Masters series curators Wayne Miller and Kevin Prufer; the staff of Pleiades Press, especially Kathryn Nuernberger; the staff of *Gulf Coast,* especially Adrienne Perry; Lucy Delap and Cole Swensen for their thoughtful consideration; the Modernist Journals Project, a joint project of Brown University and the University of Tulsa; the staff of the James C. Kirkpatrick Library at the University of Central Missouri, especially Cathy Clear; the staff of the M.D. Anderson Library at the University of Houston, especially Jesse Sharpe; Terry Wilson for his digitizing expertise; Conor Bracken for his French translations; UCM CAHSS Dean Gersham Nelson, UCM English Department Chair Daniel Schierenbeck, UH Creative Writing Chair J. Kastely, and UH English Department Chair Wyman Herendeen; Martin Rock for his extraordinary design work; and finally, but earnestly, our respective spouses, B.J. Love and Ruth Sanders.

This book is produced as a collaboration
between Pleiades Press and
Gulf Coast: A Journal of Literature and Fine Arts.

GENEROUS SUPPORT AND FUNDING PROVIDED BY:

Cynthia Woods Mitchell Center for the Arts
Houston Arts Alliance
University of Houston
Missouri Arts Council
University of Central Missouri
National Endowment for the Arts

This book is set in Adobe Caslon Pro type
with Ostrich Sans Inline and Dense titles.

Designed and typeset by Martin Rock.